"The Bolshevik Revolution
Had Descended on Me"

AMERICANS IN REVOLUTIONARY RUSSIA

Vol. 1
Albert Rhys Williams, *Through the Russian Revolution*, edited by
William Benton Whisenhunt (2016)

Vol. 2
Princess Julia Cantacuzène, Countess Spéransky, née Grant, *Russian People:
Revolutionary Recollections*, edited by Norman E. Saul (2016)

Vol. 3
Ernest Poole, *The Village: Russian Impressions*, edited by Norman E. Saul (2017)

Vol. 4
John Reed, *Ten Days That Shook the World*, edited by William Benton Whisenhunt (2017)

Vol. 5
Louise Bryant, *Six Red Months in Russia*, edited by Lee A. Farrow (2017)

Vol. 6
Edward Alsworth Ross, *Russia in Upheaval*, edited by Rex A. Wade (2017)

Vol. 7
Donald Thompson, *Donald Thompson in Russia*, edited by David H. Mould (2018)

Vol. 8
Arthur Bullard, *The Russian Pendulum: Autocracy—Democracy—Bolshevism*,
edited by David W. McFadden (2019)

Vol. 9
Pauline S. Crosley, *Intimate Letters from Petrograd*, edited by Lee A. Farrow (2019)

Vol. 10
Madeleine Z. Doty, *"The Bolshevik Revolution Had Descended on Me": Madeleine Z.
Doty's Russian Revolution*, edited by Julia L. Mickenberg (2019)

Vol. 11
David R. Francis, *Russia from the American Embassy*, edited by Vladimir V. Noskov (2019)

Vol. 12
John R. Mott, the American YMCA, and Revolutionary Russia, edited by
Matthew Lee Miller (2020)

Series General Editors:

Norman E. Saul and William Benton Whisenhunt

"The Bolshevik Revolution Had Descended on Me": Madeleine Z. Doty's Russian Revolution

Excerpted from Behind the Battle Line by
Madeleine Z. Doty

Edited and Introduction by
Julia L. Mickenberg

ANTHEM PRESS

Anthem Press
An imprint of Wimbledon Publishing Company
www.anthempress.com

First published by Slavica Publishers, Indiana University, USA, 2019

This edition first published in UK and USA 2026
by ANTHEM PRESS
75–76 Blackfriars Road, London SE1 8HA, UK
or PO Box 9779, London SW19 7ZG, UK
and
244 Madison Ave #116, New York, NY 10016, USA

Copyright © 2026 Julia L. Mickenberg editorial matter and selection;
individual chapters © individual contributors

The moral right of the authors has been asserted.

All rights reserved. Without limiting the rights under copyright reserved above,
no part of this publication may be reproduced, stored or introduced into
a retrieval system, or transmitted, in any form or by any means
(electronic, mechanical, photocopying, recording or otherwise),
without the prior written permission of both the copyright
owner and the above publisher of this book.

British Library Cataloguing-in-Publication Data
A catalogue record for this book is available from the British Library.

Library of Congress Cataloging-in-Publication Data
A catalog record for this book has been requested.

ISBN-13: 978-1-83999-752-5 (Hbk)
ISBN-10: 1-83999-752-4 (Hbk)

ISBN-13: 978-1-83999-753-2 (Pbk)
ISBN-10: 1-83999-753-2 (Pbk)

Cover design: Tracey Theriault

This title is also available as an eBook.

CONTENTS

Editor's Introduction   vii
    Julia L. Mickenberg

"THE BOLSHEVIK REVOLUTION HAD DESCENDED ON ME": MADELEINE Z. DOTY'S RUSSIAN REVOLUTION

Preface	3
I. Crossing the Pacific	5
II. Across Siberia During the Bolshevik Revolution	8
III. Turbulent Russia—Daily Life	17
IV. The Husks of Russian Royalty	25
V. Revolutionary Justice	30
VI. The Soviets—Government by the Bolsheviki	40
VII. The Germans in Petrograd	54
VIII. The Women of Russia—The Woman Comrade	69

IX. Heading Toward Home		76
Conclusion		81
Index		85

EDITOR'S INTRODUCTION
Julia L. Mickenberg

"It is a noteworthy fact that a large number of those who have written of the present situation in Russia are women," the writer Margaret Ashmun notes in a 1919 review essay entitled "Russia Through Women's Eyes":

> The modern woman does not shrink from physical hardships, and her imagination overleaps hunger and danger when she sees an issue at stake. Moreover, this is preeminently the age of woman in revolt: and whoever has the courage to rebel against oppression, in actuality or only in spirit, is an object of intense interest to women in general. Any attempt, however bungling, to right a social wrong wins from them a throb of sympathy, even when their better judgment disapproved both method and result.... This strongly developed social sense in the best type of modern woman explains why they have responded to the appeal of Russia in Revolution.[1]

Behind the Battle Line: Around the World in 1918 by Madeleine Z. Doty (1918) is among the books that Ashmun discusses, as half of that book is devoted to a discussion of the revolution unfolding in Russia. And Doty herself was in many ways the prototypical "modern woman." Today, both Doty and her account of the Russian Revolution are largely forgotten. However, Doty's own story and her reporting on the revolution, the latter drawn from *Behind the Battle Line* and reprinted here for the first time as a stand-alone volume, offer much that is of interest to contemporary readers.

Doty arrived in St. Petersburg (then called Petrograd) just days after Lenin and the Bolsheviks launched their coup against the Provisional Government, in November 1917.[2] The tsar had abdicated that March, and from that moment until the Bol-

---

[1] Margaret Ashmun, "Russia Through Women's Eyes," *The Bookman* 48, no. 6 (1919): 755–57.

[2] The Bolshevik coup began on November 7, 1917, on the Gregorian calendar. Although Doty, near the end of her life, claimed (while seeking a publisher for her autobiography) to have arrived in Petrograd just "three days after the Bolshevik Revolution," other evidence suggests that it was more like ten days after the revolution began. There is mention while she is still on the train to Petrograd of Kerensky attempting to quell the uprising, which happened Novem-

shevik coup, the Provisional Government struggled to maintain control, as Alexander Kerensky, a Socialist Revolutionary, presided over a fragile coalition of liberals and socialists, attempting to run a divided government, maintain order, and win a war while struggling to maintain the morale of a hungry and war-weary population.[3]

Doty's reporting on the Bolshevik Revolution, registering the "Alice-in-Wonderland" quality of a world suddenly turned upside down, offers a unique perspective.[4] Her descriptions are vivid, often humorous, and cover both the quotidian details of adjusting to life under the new regime as well as the machinations of an ongoing political struggle. Discussing female journalists from the West who covered the Russian Revolution, Choi Chatterjee has noted, "Women writers rarely kept a safe distance from the people they were observing; instead, they insisted on inserting themselves into the historical narrative and recording their personal experiences of the revolution."[5] As such, many women's accounts, written in first person, are not just records of the social and political transformations wrought by the revolution but also, implicitly or explicitly, narratives of personal transformation. In Doty's case, this is subtle, as she, like other visitors, grapples with discomforts, dangers, bureaucracy, and a range of inconveniences, large and small, along with fear, hope, excitement, and—after the relief of leaving Russia—finding that she can't get the place out of her mind.[6]

Doty had gone to Russia as part of an assignment for the women's magazine *Good Housekeeping*, to travel "around the world" and document the World War from the perspective of women: "What are they thinking about—the women in Russia, England, France, all the countries that have been bearing the heat and burden and sorrow of the battle these long tragic years? We have sent Miss Madeleine Doty to talk with them and find out," a promotional story in the magazine noted just as Doty was mak-

---

ber 7–11. (Kerensky, following his flight from St. Petersburg, rallied troops from Pskov and made some inroads before being defeated, forcing Kerensky into exile.) Madeleine Z. Doty, *Behind the Battle Line: Around the World in 1918* (New York: Macmillan, 1918), 35. For Doty's claim to have arrived three days after the revolution, see solicitation letter, Madeleine Z. Doty Papers, box 4, folder 35, Sophia Smith Collection, Smith College, Northampton, MA (hereafter referred to as Doty Papers). In a letter to her parents dated November 27, 1917, she mentions that she sent a cable "last week as soon as I arrived here" (Doty Papers, box 2, folder 7).

[3] The Socialist Revolutionaries grew out of populist movements in Russia and were among the "terrorist" groups that called for violence against oppressive figures in the tsarist regime. Even so, they were considered more moderate than the Social Democrats—which split into the Bolsheviks and Mensheviks—with whom they vied for power and authority.

[4] In *Behind the Battle Line*, Doty twice mentions feeling like Alice in Wonderland in Russia. It is a metaphor that was used repeatedly in accounts of the Bolshevik Revolution. Doty, *Behind the Battle Line*, 47, 68.

[5] Choi Chatterjee, "'Odds and Ends of the Russian Revolution,' 1917–1920: Gender and American Travel Narratives," *Journal of Women's History* 20, no. 4 (2008): 10–33.

[6] Comparisons to Russia occur throughout other chapters of *Behind the Battle Line*.

ing her way toward St. Petersburg. "When you read this, Miss Doty will have passed through Yokohama and Vladivostok and will be nearing the scenes of the great civil conflict in Russia," editors explain.[7] Doty sought, she tells *Good Housekeeping* readers, "to discover the dreams and plans of the women of the future, what the folks at home strove for, where the spiritual drama led."[8] The *Good Housekeeping* assignment followed on the heels of Doty's book *Short Rations: An American Woman in Germany, 1915–1916* (1917), which pulled together Doty's accounts of her earlier travels in wartime Europe. It was likewise billed as a record of "what happens at home when men go to war."[9] Touching on Doty's stops in The Hague, London, Paris, and Scandinavia, *Short Rations* focuses upon two visits to Germany, in 1915 and 1916: hence its subtitle.

In contrast, the title of *Behind the Battle Line: Around the World in 1918* is doubly misleading because half of the trip actually took place in 1917 and Russia, despite taking up half the book, is not in its title. While there are chapters on Japan, China, Russia, Sweden, Norway, France, and England, it is clear that on this trip, Russia was "at the heart of things" for Doty, just as Germany was in *Short Rations*.[10] Indeed, most reviews of the book either concentrate on the Russia chapters or make clear that these are the most interesting part of the book.[11]

Not long after Doty landed in Petrograd, she decided to extend the brief visit she'd originally planned. As she wrote to her parents, "It would be a shame not to be present at the making of history."[12] Doty stayed in Russia for nearly three months, mostly in St. Petersburg, but she also visited Moscow. Although Doty's first-person narrative of the revolution is also an account of her discomfort—and fear, and excitement, and skepticism, and many other emotional responses—she does not, in fact, foreground the "daily domestic battles" that Chatterjee says women tended to prioritize in their narratives over discussion of political events.[13] Indeed, in the Russia chapters—in contrast to other parts of the book—women are not necessarily at the center of Doty's story. Still, as Ashmun's review would suggest, Doty's feminism

---

[7] Clipping in box 1, folder 3, Doty Papers, (mis)dated in pencil January 1917. Doty did not leave on her journey until the fall of 1917, and she arrived in St. Petersburg in November (on the New Style calendar; the Russians at that time were still using the Julian calendar, so it was October there).

[8] Doty, *Behind the Battle Line*, viii.

[9] Madeleine Z. Doty, *Short Rations: An American Woman in Germany, 1915–1916* (London: Methuen, 1917), xi.

[10] Doty, *Behind the Battle Line*, viii.

[11] See "Eyewitnesses," *The Nation* (London), March 22, 1919, 756, 758; Margaret Ashmun, "Russia Through Women's Eyes," 755–57.

[12] Madeleine Doty letter to parents, November 27, 1917, box 2, folder 7, Doty Papers.

[13] Chatterjee, "'Odds and Ends of the Russian Revolution,'" 17.

made her particularly interested in the Russian Revolution, and her account offers a woman's perspective not only on some of the quotidian details of what adjustment to this "Alice-in-Wonderland" world entailed but also on "the drama of high Bolshevik politics."[14]

Although Doty had never intended to publish her account of the Russian Revolution as a stand-alone book, the fact that it was—until now—buried amidst her discussion of traveling through seven other countries diminished its impact. Notably, when Doty wrote her autobiography, she included nearly all of the Russia chapters from *Behind the Battle Line* with only minor revisions. This trip clearly represented a pivotal moment in Doty's life, for she knew she was witnessing history unfolding. Moreover, the significance of her perspective on the day-to-day experience of living in a society in upheaval is more self-evident today than it may have been before women's history became a valid field of study.[15] The Russian chapters from *Behind the Battle Line* offer a notable perspective on the Bolshevik Revolution because of Doty's background and outlook, her timing, the context in which she made her travels, and the particular events and figures she covered. Read alongside the accounts of other female journalists, such as Louise Bryant and Bessie Beatty (both of whom Doty knew and spent time with in Russia), it predicted some of the ways in which the larger number of American women who visited and worked in the Soviet Union in the decades following the revolution would respond to that experience.[16]

Madeleine Doty and the Greenwich Village Feminist Milieu

Born in New Jersey in 1877 to well-off parents, Samuel and Charlotte (Zabriskie) Doty, Madeleine Zabriskie Doty came of age at a moment in which women were increasingly gaining access to higher education and the professions, and she took full advantage of the new opportunities available to those of some means. She played an active role in the battle for women's suffrage and was a leader in the peace movement, which absorbed the attention of feminists well after women won the vote.

---

[14] Ibid., 12.

[15] An editor who rejected the manuscript of Doty's autobiography in the early 1960s called her perspective on the revolution "peripheral, not on the level of meaningful transaction." However, an archivist at Smith College, Margaret Grierson, who was eager to obtain the unpublished autobiography for Smith's archives (which are among the strongest in the world in women's history), challenged this editor's view. After quoting the editor's comments, she notes in a letter to Doty's executor, "I should suppose that the observations of the intelligent concerned woman correspondent would be of great serious value in bringing life and color and meaningful interpretation to the more official records of history." Margaret Grierson letter to Mr. Philip H. Ball, Jr., November 11, 1963, box 1, folder 1, Doty Papers.

[16] For discussion of this broader phenomenon, see Julia L. Mickenberg, *American Girls in Red Russia: Chasing the Soviet Dream* (Chicago: University of Chicago Press, 2017).

She spent her 20s and 30s living amidst the Bohemian milieu of socialists, anarchists, reformers, artists, and freethinkers in Greenwich Village, ground zero for all that was "modern" in the United States. She was a lawyer and a leader in progressive-era battles to reform prisons and the juvenile justice system, in addition to having a career as a journalist (and, much later, as a teacher). Doty's love life—most famously, her unconventional marriage to civil libertarian Roger Baldwin—put her at the forefront of new women's efforts to recast romantic relationships on a more egalitarian basis. Her interest in revolutionary Russia can be understood in relation to all these aspects of her own history.

Doty attended the exclusive Brearley School for girls in New York City and was raised in comfort: she grew up moving back and forth between New York City and the Zabriskie homestead in New Jersey, with a governess, riding lessons, and summers often spent in the exclusive upstate New York resort town of Saratoga Springs. Her family regularly traveled to Europe, and one summer Doty was promised a pony if she would learn French.[17] Although the family's fortunes had ups and downs, and Madeleine's mother suffered from mental illness, she had a relatively happy and protected childhood and youth. Doty graduated from Smith College in 1900—at a time in which less than 4 percent of all eighteen–twenty-one-year-old women attended college—and was among the even smaller minority of women who decided to pursue an independent career.[18] As Doty suggests in a 1910 article on women's colleges in the popular women's magazine *The Delineator*, the "vague longings and aspirations" that college may awaken for women usually serve little purpose in the end: "We are women and are not taught to look forward to a career. We are to be simply women. Our fulfillment lies in doing for others. So these awakened longings, these aspirations, have no result, unless perhaps they make us attend a few more prayer meetings, or fill us with resolutions of working in a college settlement when we graduate, or determinations to be a good wife and mother."[19]

Doty herself obviously had higher aspirations, attending New York University's law school after unsuccessfully attempting to take classes at Harvard, disguised as a man. "Dressed in a very simple tailored suit, with a soft felt hat pulled down over her hair, she would slip quietly into the back row, the students themselves being perfectly willing to help her conceal her identity." She managed to attend four lectures before

---

[17] Madeleine Z. Doty, *One Woman Determined to Make a Difference: The Life of Madeleine Zabriskie Doty*, ed. Alice Duffy Rinehart (Bethlehem, PA: Lehigh University Press, 2001), 35.

[18] Nancy Cott, *The Grounding of Modern Feminism* (New Haven: Yale University Press, 1987), 297. Cott is citing Barbara Solomon, *In the Company of Educated Women: A History of Women and Higher Education in America* (New Haven: Yale University Press, 1985), 64.

[19] Madeleine Z. Doty, "What a Woman's College Means to a Girl: In Most Instances It Is a Four Years' Course in Amusements, With a Little Social Training on the Side," *The Delineator*, March 1910, 209.

the professor discovered her, and she was forbidden to continue attending; hence on to New York.[20] At NYU, Doty was hardworking, serious, and apparently fairly innocent; she initially struggled socially, experiencing awkward and possibly romantic relationships with men as well as women, including a woman working at Smith College, which she visited to get a break from New York and law school. She would write, somewhat obliquely, in her autobiography, "I had learned much as a law student, many things besides the law. Among others is the relation between men and women, the meaning of sex. I had learned about the misuse of sex and the impure relation that can exist between women. I was appalled and upset."[21]

Law school ultimately set Doty on a trajectory to achieve both professional and social success, despite failure to support herself as an attorney. She became close to several women, including fellow students Crystal Eastman, Jessie Ashley, and Ida Rauh, all of whom were outspoken feminists and activists: Eastman would become New York's first female commissioner and had an important impact on New York labor law, and eventually became well-known also as a suffrage advocate and socialist. A leader in several feminist organizations and a birth control advocate, Ashley used her inherited wealth to support radical causes like amnesty for political prisoners.[22] Rauh, from a secular Jewish family, would marry Crystal's brother, Max Eastman, editor of *The Masses*, in 1905. As a founder of the Provincetown Players theater troupe, which features prominently in the Warren Beatty film *Reds* (1981), Rauh earned notoriety both for her acting and her outspoken feminism (she never actually practiced law).

Following law school and a short stint teaching in Boston, Doty returned to New York and moved into a tenement on the Lower East Side with Rauh. She, Ashley, and another friend started a law office uptown: "We hoped that a swell office uptown on Fifth Avenue would attract society women. But of course it didn't. In fact, we soon discovered that women are less ready than men to employ a woman lawyer." The costs of maintaining the office amounted to more than the women's combined income, so Doty began tutoring girls from her old school, and subsequently took up journalism.[23]

Doty had some successes as a lawyer (she became one of the first women to be made a receiver in bankruptcy cases), but in some ways it was just as well that she could not make ends meet in that professional capacity: in the few years she practiced she began to see "many injustices in the law" and was troubled by the contrast be-

---

[20] Mary B. Mullett, "Who's Who Among Progressive Women: Miss Madeleine Doty and Her Unique Experience as an Experimental Convict," *The Washington Herald*, December 22, 1913, 7.

[21] Doty, *One Woman Determined to Make a Difference*, 49.

[22] See Editors' Notes, "Ashley, Jessie, 1861–1919," http://editorsnotes.org/projects/emma/topics/90/.

[23] Doty, *One Woman Determined to Make a Difference*, 58.

tween the wealthy world of uptown and Park Avenue where her law office was located, and the poverty of the Lower East Side, where she lived.[24]

Doty and Rauh lived close to the University Settlement, a haven for wealthy male reformers and socialists, among them J. G. Phelps, the "millionaire socialist" who married the young Jewish radical Rose Pastor; William English Walling, another wealthy White Anglo-Saxon Protestant (WASP) who likewise married an immigrant Jew, Anna Strunsky; and Ernest Poole. Most men in the settlement were intensely interested in Russia; several would travel to St. Petersburg in 1905 to start a "Revolutionary News Bureau" to report on the first Russian Revolution for American readers. It was at the University Settlement that Doty "first heard about Karl Marx and socialism"; there she also could have met "the Little Grandmother of the Russian Revolution," Catherine Breshkovsky (or Breshkovskaya in Russian). Breshkovsky earned many admirers, especially among the Settlement House crowd, when she toured the United States in 1904–05 to build support for the Socialist Revolutionaries, a populist group that would later vie for authority with the Bolsheviks. (Doty's 1918 article in *Good Housekeeping* on the "Women of Russia" features a photograph of Breshkovsky, but the article's only discussion of her is a mention of the fact that Breshkovsky had apparently gone into hiding after the Bolsheviks took power.)

In the spring of 1906, after Rauh became ill with pneumonia and was taken off to Europe by her parents, Doty received an invitation to join the cooperative house on 3 Fifth Avenue known simply as "A Club." (The name arose after a reporter asked the housing collective's president what the group's name was, and he "casually replied, 'Oh, just call it a club.'") A-Club, which was bankrolled by Chicago settlement worker and factory inspector Helen Todd, housed many of the leading literary figures of the day, all of whom were "more or less radical."[25] Journalist Mary Heaton Vorse suggests that A-Club essentially functioned as "the American press bureau of the Russian 1905–1907 revolution": William English Walling and his wife, Anna Strunsky, Anna's sister Rose, Ernest Poole, Arthur Bullard, and Leroy Scott had all been to Russia to report on that first, unsuccessful revolution, and other A-Club residents, including Vorse herself, Scott's wife-to-be Miriam Finn, and Doty, would travel to Russia in the wake of the 1917 Revolution. Vorse notes, "All sorts of people from Russia came to A Club—refugees, returned travelers."

Members of A-Club were among the chief American supporters of Maxim Gorky's ill-fated visit to the United States; the scandal that erupted during his visit reveals volumes about the Victorian mores that still held sway in the 1900s, their relationship to popular conceptions of revolutionary Russia, and the extent to which

---

[24] Ibid., 59.

[25] Howard Brubaker and Charlotte Teller, quoted in Gerald W. McFarland, *Inside Greenwich Village: A New York City Neighborhood, 1898–1918* (Amherst: University of Massachusetts Press, 2001), 120–21. On Todd and Breshkovsky, see Mickenberg, *American Girls in Red Russia*, 54.

xiv "THE BOLSHEVIK REVOLUTION HAD DESCENDED ON ME"

Doty's radical milieu was out of step with most other Americans when it came to sexual morality. Along with Breshkovsky, Gorky was among a number of exiles and revolutionaries who traveled to the United States in the early 1900s to solicit support for their cause: as Doty notes of Gorky in her autobiography, "He came with his tragic story of the Czar's dictatorship and the abuse of the peasants. He told of the pogroms and the beatings and the people sent to Siberia. He came to appeal to America for aid."[26]

Figure 1. Maxim Gorky and Maria Fyodorovna Andreyevna, from Gorky's 1906 visit to the United States. Madeleine Z. Doty Papers, Sophia Smith Collection, Smith College (Northampton, MA).

---

[26] Doty, *One Woman Determined to Make a Difference*, 59–60.

Gorky was probably the most famous of the revolutionary visitors to the United States. Despite his open support for the radical Bolshevik faction of the Social Democrats, who sponsored his trip to the United States, Gorky was scheduled to be feted by many of the literary and cultural luminaries of the day, including Mark Twain, William Dean Howells, and Jane Addams. However, a scandal erupted when a newspaper revealed that Gorky's traveling companion, the acclaimed actress Madame Andreeva, was not his legal wife. Suddenly nearly all of the dinners and celebrations in Gorky's honor were cancelled, and Gorky and Andreeva were refused rooms in several hotels. But they were welcomed at A-Club, and later ferried off to stay at the Staten Island home of the Fabian socialist John Martin and his wife, friends of Doty; he also spent time at the Martins' Adirondack retreat, Summerbrook, a haven for urban intellectuals and activists.[27] "During [Gorky and Andreevna's] stay in Staten Island we spent many Sundays with them on the beach. I have vivid memories of Gorki in his long black cape and soft black hat," Doty writes. "He spoke only Russian, but Marie was his interpreter."[28]

Doty would later insist of the public shunning that "the barbarity of this treatment was unbelievable." She'd met Gorky early in his visit to the US at a reception, and credits meetings such as this—she met H. G. Wells at the same gathering—with a loosening of her inhibitions: "These people impressed me greatly. My intolerance began to drop from me. I had long since learned to smoke cigarettes and look with amusement at my former attitude. I was living a far different life from the sheltered one of the Brearley School and Smith College."[29]

It was around this time that Doty launched her journalism career: hearing that *The New York Times* was looking for a man to write book reviews, Doty "asked to be given a three-week trial without pay, saying [she] would take a man's name and no one would know the difference. They reluctantly consented, and a weekly review about books and authors began to appear under the name of 'Otis Notman,' a name they accepted though it really meant 'O 'tis not [a] man.'" Doty interviewed three or four authors a week, wrote several thousand words, and earned enough money to

---

[27] The "news" about Gorky and Andreyevna's relationship, published in the *New York World*, was not even really news, at least among "the reading public of Europe" and "most American reporters," who were part of an "off-the-record agreement" to keep the story out of the news until editors of the *World*, learning that Gorky had given exclusive rights to Hearst's *New York American*, a rival newspaper, broke the story in retaliation. See Filia Holtzman, "A Mission That Failed: Gorky in America," *Slavic and East European Journal* 6, no. 3 (1962): 227–35; Doty, *One Woman Determined to Make a Difference*, 59–60. On Summerbrook, see Richard Plunz, "City: Culture: Nature—The New York Wilderness and the Urban Sublime," in *The Urban Lifeworld: Formation, Perception, Representation* (New York: Routledge, 2005), 68.

[28] Doty, *One Woman Determined to Make a Difference*, 60.

[29] Ibid.

cover her living expenses; all of her earnings from practicing law went back into the law firm, which was still struggling.[30]

As Doty became increasingly enmeshed in the New York literary milieu, she became more involved with feminist, progressive, and socialist organizations. She was a member of the Equality League of Self-Supporting Women, a group started by Harriot Stanton Blatch (daughter of Elizabeth Cady Stanton) that promoted equal pay and women's suffrage. Blatch, who lived for two decades in England, had close ties with radical suffragettes from Britain, bringing an international focus to her organization.[31] Doty was also involved with the Intercollegiate Socialist Society and frequented the Liberal Club, "Greenwich Village's first institution for free speech," which "brought together older progressives and younger bohemians for debate and lectures."[32]

In addition, Doty was probably a member of Heterodoxy, a luncheon club for "unorthodox women" that met on alternate Saturday afternoons "for over twenty years to discuss women, literature, and politics." Heterodoxy was founded in 1912 by Marie Jenney Howe, an ordained minister and suffragist who was friendly with many of the unconventional women who lived near her in Greenwich Village, including Crystal Eastman, free love advocate Henrietta Rodman, sex educator Mary Ware Dennett, playwright Susan Glaspell, and progressive educator Elisabeth Irwin, along with other women who would become prominent figures in the suffrage movement like Inez Milholland, Rheta Childe Dorr, and Doris Stevens.[33] Heterodoxy would eventually come to include dozens of the most prominent women of the era, among them Emma Goldman's niece Stella Ballantine (Goldman herself addressed the group at least once); journalist Bessie Beatty (fellow journalist Louise Bryant went

---

[30] Ibid., 60–61.

[31] See David Dismore, "July 10, 1908: Police Intervene As Suffragists Invade Financial District," *Feminist Majority Foundation Blog*, July 10, 2014, https://feminist.org/blog/; Cott, *Grounding for Modern Feminism*, 24–25; "Equality League of Self-Supporting Women to Governor of New York," June 8, 1907, Alice Duer Miller NAWSA Suffrage Scrapbooks, 1897–1911, Library of Congress, http://memory.loc.gov/.

[32] Christine Stansell, *American Moderns: Bohemian New York and the Creation of a New Century* (New York: Metropolitan Books, 2000), 78; Peggy Lamson, *Roger Baldwin, Founder of the American Civil Liberties Union: A Portrait* (Boston: Houghton Mifflin, 1976), quoted in Duffy, "Introduction to Chapters 11–12," in Doty, *One Woman Determined to Make a Difference*, 211.

[33] Quote from Blanche Wiesen Cook, *Crystal Eastman on Women and Revolution* (New York: Oxford University Press, 1978), 13; Judith Schwarz, *Radical Feminists of Heterodoxy: Greenwich Village, 1912–1940* (Lebanon, NH: New Victoria, 1982), 9–10. Cook mentions Doty among a list of women who were members of Heterodoxy, citing Inez Haynes Irwin's papers at the Schlesinger Library; most other references I have found that mention Doty's membership cite Cook.

to at least one meeting of the group);³⁴ dancer Agnes de Mille; the sexologist Havelock Ellis's wife, Edith Ellis, who openly engaged in same-sex relationships; writers Fannie Hurst, Charlotte Perkins Gilman, Vida Scudder, Rose Pastor Stokes, Mary Heaton Vorse, and Rose Strunsky; anthropologist Elsie Clews Parsons; patron of the arts Mabel Dodge Luhan; and psychologists Leta Hollingworth and Beatrice Hinkle. Although radicals were overrepresented, the group included women of diverse political views, a number of open lesbians, and even one African American woman, Grace Nail Johnson, a National Association for the Advancement of Colored People (NAACP) activist who was married to the writer James Weldon Johnson (this at a time when nearly all aspects of American life were marked by de facto if not legal segregation).³⁵

Despite involvement in these circles, Doty's maturation as a feminist and activist—and as a woman increasingly in touch with her own sexual appetites—actually matured as she, in her words, "forsook my feminine world," spending most of her time with men. She entered into a relationship with the novelist, journalist, and muckraker David Graham Phillips after interviewing him in her Otis Notman guise. Of their relationship Doty writes, "I was to learn through suffering and anguish the meaning of love between man and woman." Phillips was drawn to Doty's independence, intelligence, and ambition, and was attracted to her physically, but he had no interest in marrying her. "And he didn't realize how immature I was, how little I knew of love and sex. He thought a woman lawyer and writer must be sophisticated. His letters troubled me." In her autobiography Doty quotes Phillips' letters, in which he professes his desire for her, suggesting that she would be betraying herself if she took the conventional route of marriage simply so that she might be able to experience the delights of physical love. As he wrote to her in January 1907:

> Certainly "it" shall be as you say. You don't suppose I would want it otherwise, do you? That garden is not a prison into which one is thrust or dragged. And I don't wonder that you are not sure you want to go there. I am disposed to think you don't. I am also disposed to think that you are deceiving yourself about your state of mind in many ways. But that's the way it is with all of us. Now, wouldn't it be quaint if what you really wanted was to stop work and all the anxieties incident to a career and secure some man, nurse your children, and superintend servants?³⁶

---

³⁴ Mary Dearborn, *Queen of Bohemia: The Life of Louise Bryant* (New York: Houghton Mifflin, 1996), 44. Dearborn mentions that Bryant's friend Sara Bard Field brought her to a Heterodoxy meeting, and that "through Heterodoxy she made friends, among them Madeleine Doty, another journalist" (ibid., 45).

³⁵ Schwarz, *Radical Feminists of Heterodoxy*, 86–94.

³⁶ Doty, *One Woman Determined to Make a Difference*, 60. Quotations from 62, 64.

Doty would eventually give herself completely—in the physical sense—to Phillips, but his wish to have ongoing intimate relations without marriage was intolerable to her, in part because she seems to have gotten pregnant with Phillips' child.[37] Early on in their relationship, Doty developed gastrointestinal problems that would plague her for the rest of her life, and though she recognized that her physical discomforts came from struggles to control her own "passionate nature," this knowledge did not make the problem any easier to bear. "He wanted me to agree that a secret relation without marriage was right. This I was never able to do."[38] Their tormented relationship lasted on and off for a number of years until Phillips was shot and killed by a mentally ill man. Phillips would be one of the two great loves in Doty's life.

Bolshevik attitudes about sex (that it was a private matter; that abortion, though discouraged, should be legal and free; and that no child could be considered "illegitimate") were appealing to significant numbers of modern women from the United States. Doty never commented in her writings on the topic, even when reporting on her interview with Alexandra Kollontai, chief spokesperson for some of the Bolsheviks' most radical challenges to morality. At the time of Doty's writings about Russia, her own attitudes concerning sex were likely still unresolved.

At the time of Phillips' death, Doty had been working for nearly a year on a child-welfare exhibit for the City of New York, focusing on the courts and delinquent children.[39] As part of this work, Doty traveled throughout the United States to gather material; in St. Louis she met Roger Baldwin, who at the time was chief probation officer: "As I talked with him I little thought that this very attractive young man would one day become my husband."[40] Because of Doty's work on the child welfare exhibit the Russell Sage Foundation hired her as executive secretary of a new Juvenile Court Committee "to reform conditions in New York." Doty's growing notoriety as a social investigator and reformer brought a new urgency to her career as a journalist, as she

---

[37] A letter in her files from one of Doty's Boston doctors, dated October 9 (with no year, but 1911 is penciled on the letter in Doty's files), notes "your daughter was operated on" and "survived" (quoted in Duffy, "Addendum," in Doty, *One Woman Determined to Make a Difference*, 258). As Duffy notes, "A lady did not admit to an illegitimate birth in those days. And Doty was a lady; by not telling she protected the man's reputation and her own." No further information is available about when the child was born or what happened to her.

[38] Doty, *One Woman Determined to Make a Difference*, 73.

[39] In this sense, Doty was like "progressive maternalists" who gained public authority through child-related reform work in the early twentieth century. See Molly Ladd Taylor, *Mother-Work: Women, Child Welfare, and the State, 1890–1930* (Urbana: University of Illinois Press, 1994).

[40] Doty, *One Woman Determined to Make a Difference*, 75. Baldwin himself says that they met at a national conference of social work in 1912, after he'd just left a job in the St. Louis juvenile court; his account seems to imply that they met in New York City. Roger N. Baldwin, "A Memo on Madeleine Zabriskie Doty for the files at Smith College," October 1978, box 1, folder 4, Doty Papers.

gave up her law practice completely: "My dream of being a great woman lawyer, a Portia, seemed a silly dream. I was afraid. Afraid I would never be able to earn my living," she recalled later.[41]

Through her work on the juvenile court system, Doty became a major force in prison reform more generally. She came to conclude that harsh treatment of juvenile delinquents had the effect of increasing (rather than decreasing) recidivism. Doty played an active role in the creation of a separate juvenile court system in New York City, began writing exposés for the popular press, and was appointed a New York State Prison commissioner, "without a salary but with full liberty to investigate all prisons and reformatories."[42] Doty and a friend spent two weeks under cover, living in the State Prison for Women in Auburn, posing as Maggie Martin and Lizzie Watson, check forgers. The exposés Doty published in magazines and newspapers caused a sensation. These articles, along with a discussion of the relationship between the juvenile justice system and adult criminality—based on extensive interviews—formed the basis of her first book, *Society's Misfits*, a stunning critique of the prison system, based on inside experience, that led to important reforms. As Doty reflected later:

> The whole prison system seemed based on stupidity and ignorance. With a little common sense the physical if not the spiritual aspect could be transformed in a day. As it is, hundreds of working people are given into the state's care and are taught nothing, produce nothing, are ill-housed and ill-fed. Their time and that of the guards or keepers is wasted. The result is an organization which manufactures criminals, and is maintained at great cost to the state.[43]

Society's Misfits was published in 1916, but by then Doty was already well known. She had gotten to know prominent men (not just Gorky and Phillips, but also Theodore Dreiser, Theodore Roosevelt, John Galsworthy, Judge Ben Lindsey, and others) and her writings were widely read. A sketch of her published in *The Washington Herald* in December of that year offers a striking portrait:

> Miss Doty is young and attractive. The look out of her clear blue eyes is fearless. She is tremendously in earnest, but with it all she has a keen sense of humor. In fact, she seems to have a keen sense of everything. That is the dominant impression she makes on you—that she is intensely alive, absorbed in the vital things of today.
>
> For so young a woman she has had a remarkable experience and she means to use it in bettering social and industrial conditions, especially as they affect

---

[41] Doty, *One Woman Determined to Make a Difference*, 74–75.

[42] Ibid., 92.

[43] Ibid., 105; Madeleine Z. Doty, *Society's Misfits* (New York: Century, 1916), 52.

women and children. But she isn't likely to find many ways of doing this as picturesque as her convict experience was.[44]

Doty's undercover journalism fit squarely into a tradition of "girl stunt reporters" that stretched back to the late 1880s, when Nellie Bly feigned insanity to go undercover as a mental patient in the insane asylum on Blackwell's Island, hitting upon "a strategy that transformed her own white, middle-class body into a vehicle of publicity that anchored her pursuit of 'the real' in corporeal experience."[45] Unlike Bly and others of her ilk, Doty's goal was not sensationalism but social change, and in this she had significant successes, both in helping individuals she came to know through her research and in instituting systemic changes in the New York penal system.

Doty's realization that she could better support herself as a journalist than as a lawyer or bureaucrat coincided with the onset of World War I, which dramatically shifted her attention to the cause of peace. That cause would preoccupy her for the rest of her life.

Peace Activism

Even as Doty became increasingly involved in the movement for women's suffrage (see figure 2), she connected this work with efforts to achieve peace, joining the American Union Against Militarism as well as the Women's Peace Party (WPP), both of which were founded by friend Crystal Eastman. In *Peace as a Women's Issue*, Harriet Hyman Alonso suggests that the historic link between peace and women's rights activism comes from a connection that women have made between violence against women and institutionalized violence. Essentialist ideas about women as naturally more nurturing and caring "and more committed to producing a humanistic and compassionate world than men as a whole" were also widely accepted in Doty's time. The notion that all women were natural mothers or metaphorical mothers to the world also suggested a feminine responsibility to counter men's violent tendencies; in the vision of a new world that "women's rights peace activists" imagined, women would "play a key role … no longer the abused, exploited, and angry outsiders, but rather the creative, productive, and nurturing insiders."[46] Doty joined other women in speaking against the prominent English suffragist, Christabel Pankhurst, when

---

[44] Mullett, "Who's Who Among Progressive Women."

[45] Jean Marie Lutes, *Front Page Girls: Women Journalists in American Culture and Fiction, 1880–1930* (Ithaca, NY: Cornell University Press, 2006), 15.

[46] Harriet Hyman Alonso, *Peace As a Women's Issue: A History of the U.S. Movement for World Peace and Women's Rights* (Syracuse, NY: Syracuse University Press, 1993), 11.

she came to the United States urging women to support the allied war effort.[47] After seeing Alla Nazimova's moving performance in *War Brides* (a play about newlywed women having to send their husbands off to war), Doty decided to gather other peace activists to stand outside the theater "after each performance and pass out to each red-eyed woman literature calculated to crystalize her emotion into action which will make such scenes she has just seen enacted impossible."[48] Beyond distributing material for the WPP, Doty joined about seventy-five other members of the group, among them Settlement House pioneer Jane Addams, doctor Alice Hamilton, child welfare advocate Grace Abbott, and economist and sociologist Emily Balch, for the first Women's International Peace Convention at The Hague, where the Women's International League for Peace and Freedom (WILPF) would be founded.

Figure 2. Doty in suffrage parade (standing beside woman carrying "lawyers" sign), undated. Madeleine Z. Doty Papers, Sophia Smith Collection, Smith College (Northampton, MA).

---

[47] "American and English Suffragists and Antis Denounce Miss Christabel Pankhurst's Recruiting Campaign in America," *New-York Tribune*, January 15, 1915, 9.

[48] "Some Women Sniffed, and the Peace Movement Received Sudden Impetus," *New-York Tribune*, February 3, 1915, 7.

After the United States entered the war, Doty made direct links between war and the need for women's suffrage. As she told a Senate committee in 1917, in a state of war woman needed the vote so "that she may conserve the prosperity of her country, keep freedom alive in the land and permit no deterioration of those ideals of social service which have been established." Indeed, she added, "If we are really sincere in our declaration that we are fighting for the freedom of the people then let us prove it by an act so democratic that even German autocracy cannot deny our sincerity. Let us grant the suffrage now and at once to all the women of America."[49]

World Travel and Marriage

Doty had opened her book *Short Rations* with an account of her journey to The Hague, where Doty would be among the founders of WILPF. The news articles that she published about this trip—and her travels through Germany, France (where she served briefly as a nurse), and England—brought her renown as a credible source for news of the war's effects on the home front, and she subsequently returned to Germany, bringing supplies for war orphans as her cover. *Short Rations* describes all of these travels. However, Doty's open peace advocacy brought an avalanche of criticism once the United States entered the war. Luckily for Doty, it was before this shower of criticism really commenced that *Good Housekeeping* sent her on the trip "round the world" that would fortuitously drop her into the midst of the Bolshevik Revolution.

Behind the Battle Line would be Doty's last published book, although she continued publishing articles for a number of years, and after she moved to Geneva in 1925, where she lived out much of her life, she served as editor of *Pax International*, the journal of the WILPF, from 1925 to 1931. She also served as the league's international secretary. Prior to that time, and inseparable from her travels to and return from revolutionary Russia (where a new ideal of comradely love had been articulated by women like Kollontai), Doty fell in love with Roger Baldwin. The two married in 1919 in a small ceremony in the woods with vows that became legendary for the new ideal they embodied. "We deny without reservation the whole conception of property in marriage," they declared, rejecting "the whole Puritan philosophy of life" and framing their union as a contribution to the cause of "the great revolutionary struggle for human freedom, so intense, so full of promise today."[50] Doty kept her name after marriage and showed no interest in giving up her career, contrary to usual practice at that time.

Doty and Baldwin's "50-50" arrangement of sharing all household expenses and refusing to value one person's work or social commitments over another's, which

---

[49] Madeleine Doty, "Voteless Women in Warring Europe," *The Suffragist*, May 5, 1917, 7. [A speech delivered before the Senate committee on April 26, 1917.]

[50] Madeleine Z. Doty and Roger Baldwin marriage vows, box 1, folder 4, Doty Papers.

echoed Soviet practice, was as idealistic as it was ultimately unsustainable: Baldwin "paid" Doty when she took over housework after they had to let go of the maid, and although their arrangement made for good media fodder, eventually the independent lives each partner led proved divisive.[51] Although they'd met five years earlier, Doty and Baldwin formed a real connection when their paths crossed again in 1917 through peace activism after Baldwin replaced Crystal Eastman as director of the American Union Against Militarism. Years later, Baldwin recalled of meeting Doty that he was "attracted to Madeleine at once." He described her as "the rare type of independent professional woman, feminist, socialist, but not radical in a revolutionary sense, a writer in the national magazines, and a lawyer who did not practice, or had only briefly. She was like me essentially a social reformer. I was attracted also by her gayety and humor, her clear blue eyes, her trim figure and her professional women's style of dressing."[52] Although it was peace activism that brought them together, Baldwin and Doty's shared interest in Russia cemented their bond: "He was thrilled with the struggle of the Russian people for freedom," Doty wrote later. "I was full of my experiences in Russia."[53] Although within months after Doty's return from Russia the two would decide to marry, the marriage was delayed by Baldwin's imprisonment for refusing to be drafted into the military.

Once they were finally able to be together, their years of happiness turned out to be brief, as Baldwin and Doty wound up spending too much time on their own work (Baldwin was a founder of the American Civil Liberties Union) and not enough time nurturing their relationship. Doty had an abortion early on in their marriage (she was 40 by this time), and the two drifted apart emotionally and eventually physically. When Doty left for Geneva in 1925 their marriage was essentially over. They formally divorced in 1935, but stayed in touch until Doty's death in 1963, and despite their "50-50" ideal, Doty relied on Baldwin for assistance financially.[54]

In Geneva, Doty worked with various peace organizations, started a Smith College year abroad in Geneva program, and obtained her PhD. She taught for several years at a girls' school in Florida so she would qualify for social security benefits in the US, and then obtained another teaching position back in Geneva, where she re-

---

[51] See, for instance, "Married Life on Fifty-fifty Basis Succeeds," *Grand Forks Herald* (ND), September 20, 1920, 16.

[52] Roger Baldwin, "A Memo on Madeleine Zabriskie Doty for the files at Smith College."

[53] Doty, *One Woman Determined to Make a Difference*, 213.

[54] "Even on my small income I had been helping her out," Baldwin writes. "She had never made demands on me but when it came to divorce she had wanted far more than I could give. So we settled on a joint sum of $5000 to which I contributed half for her to draw on as needed. We had gone along 50-50 in our married years while she worked, as she did most of the time, and wanted to, but I helped when she was between jobs" (Baldwin, "A Memo on Madeleine Zabriskie Doty for the files at Smith College").

mained until the last year of her life. She returned to the United States in the spring of 1963 and moved into a retirement home in the Berkshires, where she died six months later.

Women Writing the Russian Revolution

When Doty arrived in St. Petersburg in November 1918, a number of female journalists from the United States—just about all of them active in the suffrage movement—were already in Petrograd. As Chris Dubbs notes in his study of American journalists reporting on World War I, echoing Ashmun's review essay from a century prior:

> Those journalists who championed social causes such as labor reform and women's suffrage, who fought against poverty, political corruption, and social privilege were inspired by the birth of democracy in Russia. Conspicuous among them was the largest group of female reporters ever assembled in the war. Most could not be labeled as war correspondents. They had cut their journalistic teeth by exposing corruption in government and the exploitation of women and workers. They felt in sympathy with the socialistic values of the revolution and its provisional government.[55]

A few of these women, like Florence Harper, had gone to Russia to report on the war and found themselves in the midst of revolution; this might be said of Doty as well, but she was less interested in reporting on the war itself than on the war's impact, and she was eager, at least at first, to watch the Russian Revolution unfold.

Rheta Childe Dorr, a prominent member of the National Woman's Party and editor of the *The Suffragist*, left Russia not long before Doty arrived; although Dorr had been eager to see a new, democratic Russia, she was even more critical of the Bolsheviks, and fearful of their violent tendencies.[56] Louise Bryant and Bessie Beatty's accounts of the Bolshevik Revolution are better remembered today than Doty's in large part because Doty's discussion is buried amid the other chapters of *Behind the Battle Line*, and the book's title makes no reference to Russia or the revolution. Beatty and Bryant also stayed in Russia for a longer period and were able to discuss the impact of both the February and October Revolutions: Beatty arrived in St. Petersburg early in the summer of 1917 and Bryant arrived in September; all three women left Russia together in February 1918. (Warren Beatty's *Reds*, which focuses on Bryant

---

[55] Chris Dubbs, *American Journalists in the Great War: Rewriting the Rules of Reporting* (Lincoln: University of Nebraska Press, 2017), 180.

[56] Rheta Childe Dorr, *Inside the Russian Revolution* (New York: Macmillan, 1917).

and her husband John Reed as chroniclers of the Russian Revolution, also contributed to Bryant's longevity as a public figure.)[57]

As historian Lynn Dumenil notes, "The chaotic conditions meant that intrepid male and female reporters had unusual opportunities to report the extraordinary events, such as the storming of the Winter Palace in Petrograd that unfolded as the Bolsheviks solidified their power."[58] The intensity and proximity of events that women like Beatty, Bryant, and Doty reported are striking, though striking too are some of the subtle differences in the way they did so. Beatty and Bryant were both younger than Doty when they came to Russia: Beatty was thirty-one and Bryant was thirty-two, while Doty was nearly forty. This slight generational difference may have had some impact on their perspectives. All three women had some association with the feminist group Heterodoxy; all were active in the suffrage struggle; and all were relatively sympathetic to the revolution, though Bryant was more actively pro-Bolshevik than the other two.

In comparing the three women's accounts of the revolution, Doty seems somewhat less intrepid, despite the fact she, like Beatty, traveled to Russia on her own (Bryant traveled with her husband, John Reed). Indeed, in multiple instances throughout Doty's writings, it is clear that, her reputation and history as an independent woman and feminist notwithstanding, she relied heavily upon men to help her: in Harbin she was aided by a man "in European dress" who helped her find the British Consulate; on the train to Siberia, she was aghast at having been asked to share a sleeping compartment with a Cossack soldier and she was relieved when a group of English-speaking businessmen traveling for an American firm offered to give up one of their compartments so that Doty could have a berth to herself. One of these businessmen essentially adopted Doty after she became ill, continuing to care for her once they arrived in St. Petersburg; indeed, although she does not acknowledge this in the text of *Behind the Battle Line* itself, other versions of her account make it clear that it is from this man, Nick, that her initial account of the Bolshevik coup was taken.[59]

---

[57] Virginia Gardner, *"Friend and Lover": The Life of Louise Bryant* (New York: Horizon Press, 1982), 125. Several sources repeat reference to the three women traveling together. However, Doty's "Women of the Future" article in *Good Housekeeping* (which Gardner cites) and books by all three women imply that each woman traveled alone. Bryant's testimony before the Overman Committee does suggest she knew that Doty and Beatty had, like her, agreed to serve as couriers for the Bolsheviks, which would give some indication that they traveled together. See "Bolshevik Propaganda: Hearings Before a Subcommittee of the Committee on the Judiciary, United States Senate, Sixty-fifth Congress, third session and thereafter, pursuant to S. Res. 439 and 469, February 11, 1919 to March 10, 1919," https://archive.org.

[58] Lynn Dumenil, *The Second Line of Defense: American Women and World War I* (Chapel Hill: University of North Carolina Press, 2017), 142.

[59] Madeleine G. [sic] Doty, "Among the Bolsheviks II—Petrograd," *The Nation* (London), April 20, 1918, 60–62.

Doty's distress at the violence unleashed by the revolution is also a striking aspect of her narrative. Like both Bryant and Beatty, she initially found many things to admire about what she discovered in revolutionary Russia. Even in the eerie silence of her landing in St. Petersburg, she was impressed by people's eagerness to talk, to argue, to engage: "Everywhere there was movement and action, but no violence." She writes:

> People stopped to argue. Voices rose high and arms waved wildly. It was a people intensely alive and intensely intelligent. Every one had an opinion. It was my first glimpse of Russia. My heart leaped up. These people had not been contaminated by proximity to German militarism. They were not cogs in a machine. In spite of suppression they were not servile. They were alive and free. Continually that first impression was verified. Every Russian I met could talk. Those who couldn't read or write could talk.[60]

Besides this, simply being there was exciting: "There was one great joy about life in Russia. It was thrillingly interesting. You could not be bored." In her article in *The Atlantic*, Doty describes the particular relish with which she experienced at least one of the new Bolshevik decrees: "Every day the Bolsheviks issued some new decree. One day all titles were abolished; the next, judges and lawyers were eliminated. They and their knowledge were deemed to be useless. I confess to a wicked delight on that occasion. I am a lawyer and know how little justice there often is in the law."[61] She was critical of the Bolsheviks' violent methods, but recognized their sincerity and their appeal and frequently notes finding their lack of airs and general informality refreshing. As to their appeal, she describes the way in which she herself was involuntarily swept up by Lenin's presence and words when she first heard him speak:

> He started in like a college professor reading a lecture. He didn't pound or rant. But in a few minutes the crowd was still. His words burnt in. Each one came liquid clear. It was like a stream that started small and grew to a deep swift running river. The man was sincere, a fanatic, but an idealist. I found myself swept along, throbbing and beating with every emotion of the great rough peasants. My reason was against what was being done. I didn't believe in winning by force. I believed in democracy. I believed everyone should have a voice. The bourgeoisie were not all bad, nor the proletariat all good.... Not a class conscious but a world conscious decision of right was what was needed.

---

[60] Doty, *Behind the Battle Line*, 40.

[61] Madeleine Z. Doty, "Revolutionary Justice," *The Atlantic*, July 1918, 129–39.

Yet in spite of my belief I found myself shouting and clamoring with the left. It was infectious.[62]

Doty had ambivalent feelings about both the Bolsheviks and the Russian bourgeoisie. Although Beatty acknowledged that she'd have preferred the moderates who supported Kerensky, she nonetheless ends her account of the revolution, *The Red Heart of Russia* (1918), by insisting, "To have failed to see the hope in the Russian Revolution is to be as a blind man looking at a sunrise."[63] In contrast, although Doty would say that Russians deserved Americans' support, she nonetheless expressed hope that more moderate forces would ultimately replace them. As she notes in a piece she wrote for *The Nation* (London), much of which is included in *Behind the Battle Line*, "When I went to Russia I was keen on revolution; but, having seen one, I didn't want any more—at least not bloody ones conducted by brute force."[64] Or, as she puts it in the book, "The working class fought for power and became dictators. They rule not by the vote, but by force. They pulled existence down to the conditions of the poorest workingman. They failed to live up to their ideals of beauty, brotherhood, fair play and freedom."[65]

On a train to Moscow, Doty sat with a Russian woman who was wearing a Red Cross uniform. Early in their journey, in a striking scene of female solidarity, Doty, her interpreter, and the Russian woman blocked the door of their cabin to keep a Russian merchant from taking the unoccupied berth in their compartment, after which the women all got to talking. The Russian woman admitted she was a member of the former aristocracy, in disguise to protect herself. All her family's land and belongings had been seized. Her husband, formerly an officer in the army, was now a common soldier. And once the cash she had on hand ran out she would probably have to work as a domestic. "Again I had a bewildered sense of a turned upside down world," Doty remarks. "I felt I ought to hurry back to New York and get the Charity Organization Society to do work among the nobility."[66] However, not all of the former nobility seemed to Doty to be worthy of such sympathy or charity. At a trial for a monarchist and reactionary, Vladimir Purishkevich, Doty was appalled by a group of very obviously wealthy women who entered the courtroom four hours after her and expected Doty to move to the back of the room so that they, relatives of the defendant, could have her spot. The woman "reddened with anger" when Doty refused:

---

[62] Doty, *Behind the Battle Line*, 92.

[63] Bessie Beatty, *The Red Heart of Russia* (New York: Century, 1919), 480.

[64] Doty, "Among the Bolsheviks II," 62.

[65] Doty, *Behind the Battle Line*, 49.

[66] Ibid., 53.

> Her insolence was intolerable. She seemed to have forgotten that there had been a revolution. She planted herself half on me and half on the bench. She was very beautiful, but her body was as hard and rigid as her face. I found my temper mounting. I understood the rage of the Bolsheviki at the insolence of the autocracy. I drove my elbow with a vicious dig into the young woman. She grew furious, but she no longer had the power to order me to a dungeon.[67]

Doty adds that she wound up sitting between these "duchesses" and a couple of cooks who had come straight from a kitchen, their arms covered in grease. Still, "of the two, the cooks had better manners."[68]

That Doty could be critical of Bolshevik methods but still empathize with their rage at the aristocracy helps bring balance to her discussion; so, too, the perspective she had on Germany—having recently spent significant time there—made her chapter on peace negotiations with Germany one of the richest in the book. Most notable here is her attention to certain particulars of the negotiations—especially the visit of a German delegation to Petrograd—that receive little attention in books by writers who were in Russia longer than Doty and thus probably had too many other things to report on. Striking in this chapter is her account of gaining entry to a meeting in the Alexandrinsky Theater in Petrograd. Using a combination of incomprehension and patience that finally frustrated the soldier on guard, Doty was taken through a back door and then actually led across the stage in front of Trotsky, Spiridonova, Kollontai, and other Bolshevik leaders before finding her seat with members of the press: "Each moment I expected to hear jeers from the gallery," she writes. "But the Russian is used to eccentricities and informalities. No one paid the slightest heed to us."[69]

Doty's ambivalent feelings about the Bolsheviks, her strongly negative view of German militarism, and her hidebound commitment to peace all came into conflict in Doty's discussion of the German peace negotiations. In Germany, Doty had made strong connections with Social Democrats like Clara Zetkin and Karl Liebknecht, who had ties to the Bolsheviks in Russia. And as a pacifist, she could certainly appreciate the Bolsheviks' desire for peace. But she blamed the Bolsheviks for having signed "undemocratic peace terms," suggesting that "had the Russians had the faith to refuse" to sign these terms, "the war might have been over today."[70] Beatty, in contrast, blamed the Allies for refusing to support the Bolsheviks in their negotiations, despite her stated belief that Russia ought to have stayed in the war: "What the Russian did not know was that his brothers in Germany are themselves enslaved to the military

---

[67] Ibid., 68.

[68] Ibid.

[69] Ibid., 102.

[70] Ibid., 118.

ideal, and that the only way to win freedom is to defeat them and the power that keeps them in bondage. He did not realize that the only way to give constructive Germany back to the world is to destroy destructive Germany."[71] As Beatty notes in a chapter entitled "The Great Betrayal": "The Russians were blind to the true character of the men who came to Brest-Litovsk to negotiate a Kaiser's peace; but the blindness of those Russian dreamers was lucid vision as compared with the blindness of the enlightened democratic world as to the real significance of the various forces at work upon the Russian tragedy." Beatty adds, "We will pay for that blindness—we must pay—for democracy is not safe in the world while Russia is enslaved. No settlement of the international situation will be lasting that does not leave the peoples of Russia free to work out their own democratic salvation." The Germans, Beatty says, had successfully driven a wedge between the Russians and their real allies, and this was the greatest betrayal.[72]

Doty did not blame the Allies, and although she was critical of the peace terms that the Bolsheviks signed, she makes clear that they did not make peace with Germany out of any pro-German feeling, but out of necessity. Doty concludes, "It is not Germany that will conquer Russia, it is Russia that will revolutionize Germany."[73] Lenin had erroneously made this very argument, expecting a German revolution would quickly follow on the heels of Russia's making a peace treaty between the two countries no longer necessary. Negotiations to get Russia out of the war were stalled further by Trotsky's insistence that if the Bolsheviks simply refused to keep fighting without signing a treaty they could have peace on their own terms. Trotsky's "no war no peace" strategy, a failed attempt to pull Russia out of the war while refusing to make peace on German terms, ended up forcing the Bolsheviks to sign a treaty even less desirable than they'd originally been offered after a predicted revolution in Germany failed to materialize and German troops approaching Petrograd called Trotsky's bluff.[74] Although Doty echoed the Bolshevik position on Germany's revolutionary potential, she criticized Bolshevik hypocrisy in dealing with their own people, noting that "the idealist must preach with clean hands," and condemning "suppression of the press, the arrest of moderate socialists," and other acts of intolerance that the Bolsheviks displayed.[75]

Despite Doty's outspoken opposition to "German autocracy" (and her criticism of the Bolsheviks' treatment of those who challenged their authority), she was not im-

---

[71] Beatty, *Red Heart of Russia*, 89.

[72] Ibid., 473.

[73] Doty, *Behind the Battle Line*, 118.

[74] John W. Wheeler-Bennett, *Brest-Litovsk: The Forgotten Peace, March 1918* (New York: W. W. Norton, 1938), 137, 207–39.

[75] Ibid., 117.

mune from prejudices that would make Germany the world's leader in promulgating racist hatreds. Doty's vision of herself as a "Portia" cannot be separated from the anti-Semitic connotations of this character in Shakespeare's *The Merchant of Venice*: Disguised as a man, Portia plays the role of a lawyer's apprentice who uses her impressive knowledge of the law to outwit her unjust father, a character often referred to in the play as simply "the Jew." In her autobiography, Doty mentions the unpleasant smell emitted by the "Russian German Jews" from the Lower East Side in her law school class, and in some versions of her reporting on Russia she identifies a rude Russian man on the train to St. Petersburg as a "little Jew."[76]

Such prejudices were not unusual for women in Doty's milieu. In *The Feminist Avant-Garde*, Lucy Delap makes clear that anti-Semitism "was a theme widely expressed and discussed within the feminist intellectual community" in both Britain and the United States in the early twentieth century. But Delap points to the "complexity of such a discourse, which could be both progressive and conservative, and sometimes quite friendly to Jewish 'emancipation.'"[77] Indeed, a significant number of American feminists were active in campaigns for "Russian freedom" that exploded following the Kishinev Massacre in 1903, one of a series of anti-Jewish pogroms. In Kishinev, a Russian city in the Pale of Settlement (to which Jews were restricted under the tsar), hundreds of Jews were killed or badly injured, over a thousand Jewish homes and over 500 Jewish businesses were destroyed.[78] Thus, although mistreatment of (Russian) Jews, along with that of African Americans, provided direct inspiration for feminist activism (the first women's movement grew directly out of abolitionist activism among women), Jews were also associated with qualities that feminists tended to reject. According to Delap, "The frequently feminized qualities of 'the Jew'—imitative, parasitic, and uncreative—corresponded to those of 'bondwomen,' and was therefore a rhetorical device to indicate dislike of capitalism and a critique of conventional femininity."[79]

Revolutionary Women

Perhaps the most striking difference between Doty's accounts and those of Beatty and Bryant is that despite Doty's ostensible mission of studying the situation of women during the war, she gives Russian women surprisingly little attention. This can likely be best explained by the fact that, landing in the midst of a revolution, and with

---

[76] Doty, *One Woman Determined to Make a Difference*, 43.

[77] Lucy Delap, *The Feminist Avant-Garde: Transatlantic Encounters of the Early Twentieth Century* (New York: Cambridge University Press, 2007), 277.

[78] See Philip Ernest Schoenberg, "The American Reaction to the Kishinev Pogrom of 1903," *American Jewish Historical Quarterly* 63, no. 3 (1974); Mickenberg, *American Girls in Red Russia*, 45.

[79] Delap, *Feminist Avant-Garde*, 278.

limited time, Doty apparently felt compelled to devote her attention to where it seemed the real action was. As she notes in an article in *The Nation*, "I had come to study Russian women, to find out their hopes and plans for the future. But in the turbulent struggle hopes and plans had temporarily disappeared. The women were down to rock bottom. They stood in line and struggled for food and clothes for the family. It was they who ran the cars and tended the switches. It was they who worked in the stores and cleaned the houses. Without them the world could not have gone on."[80] This is an important acknowledgment, but by saying little about women apart from the points she makes in her chapter on "The Women of Russia—The Woman Comrade," she implies that women were not, in fact, at the core of all the action.

Beatty, in some sense, suggests this too, starting her chapter on "Women in the Revolution" by stating outright, "there was no feminist movement in Russia," words almost identical to Doty's claim that there is "no feminist group" in Russia. Recent scholarship by Rochelle Ruthchild challenges this claim, suggesting that while activists on behalf of women's rights did not use the term "feminism," significant "women's rights victories" were achieved in conjunction with "Russia's twentieth century revolutions."[81] Notwithstanding, Beatty's account of the gender distribution at an important political meeting in St. Petersburg is striking, encompassing a critique of gender dynamics in the Western world as well:

> Here, as elsewhere, governmental honors were largely to the male; but the mundane business of making the world of meat and drink was largely left to women. Women in Russia do what women of the Western world do. At the big democratic convention in the Alexandrinski Theater, I counted the number of seats occupied by women. There were sixteen hundred delegates and twenty-three of them were women. Many other women were in evidence, but they were behind the samovars, serving tea and caviar and sausage sandwiches. Some wore red armbands, ushered the men to their seats, took stenographic reports of proceedings, and counted ballots. It was so natural that it almost made me homesick.[82]

Doty claims that "the Russian woman is a man in petticoats" who "hasn't given her life to personal service and social welfare, but to man's fight for polit-

---

[80] Doty, "Among the Bolsheviks II," 62.

[81] Rochelle Goldberg Ruthchild, *Equality & Revolution: Women's Rights in the Russian Empire, 1905–1917* (Pittsburgh: University of Pittsburgh Press, 2010), 10.

[82] Beatty, *Red Heart of Russia*, 358.

ical freedom."[83] However, Beatty's further discussion suggests that Doty's insistence that in Russia "woman was [nothing more than] man's comrade and mate," and her "womanhood had been cast from her for the sake of revolution," says more about Doty's own assumptions and biases than it does about Russian women.[84] Doty is correct to assert that "it is as revolutionists that Russian women are famous," but Russian women's striking visibility in revolutionary struggles, going back to the 1870s, had made them legendary in the United States, and had attracted many American women to the cause of Russian freedom. Doty says that "[the Russian woman] did not seek to express herself but instead adopted man's methods in the fight for freedom."[85] Beatty, instead of suggesting that Russian women are unwomanly, rationalizes the absence of a separatist feminism in Russia by pointing out that with nearly all of the people oppressed, Russian women, instead of fighting for women's rights in particular, had historically fought alongside men for basic human rights: "In the days of the terrorists," Beatty writes, "women claimed the right to throw bombs as well as men. It was granted them. With equal generosity, the government rewarded them with hard labor, exile in Siberia, and even hanging. They spent their strength and their blood as lavishly, as recklessly, as courageously, as any of their brother Nihilists."[86]

Most notably, in contrast to Bryant and Beatty, Doty fails to comment on the elements of the Bolshevik program—already being implemented while she was there—that would attract hundreds of Western women to the Soviet Union in coming years. Like Beatty and Bryant, Doty interviewed Alexandra Kollontai and Maria Spiridonova—the two leading Bolshevik women—and she reported on the trial of the liberal Countess Panina, Kollontai's predecessor as minister of welfare, who was imprisoned and tried under the Bolsheviks for refusing to turn over funds that she'd raised for Noradnyi Dom, a library and social hall created for the benefit of St. Petersburg workers. (Doty was more sympathetic to Panina than Bryant, who reported a young workingwoman's comment: "Panina really does like poor people—she thinks they are almost as good as other people.")[87] Doty missed the opportunity to speak to Catherine Breshkovsky, who had already gone into hiding by the time she arrived. And despite the fact that Doty spoke with both Kollontai and Spiridonova, her portraits of both of these women are very short and give the impression that she did not manage to establish a real rapport with either.

Unlike Beatty and Bryant, Doty also does not discuss the early interventions made by Kollontai to revolutionize women's position in Russia, beginning with paid

---

[83] Doty, *Behind the Battle Line*, 119–29.

[84] Ibid., ix.

[85] For further discussion, see chapter 1 of Mickenberg, *American Girls in Red Russia*.

[86] Beatty, *Red Heart of Russia*, 357.

[87] Louise Bryant, *Six Red Months in Russia* (New York: George H. Doran, 1918), 122.

maternity leave before and after women gave birth, time off from work for nursing infants, and a "Palace of Motherhood" designed to educate women about maternal health and hygiene. Within a few years after the revolution, according to the historian Wendy Goldman, Soviet marriage laws and family policies "constituted nothing less than the most progressive family legislation the world had ever seen," making women equal under the law, simplifying divorce, ending the category of illegitimate children, giving women property rights, legalizing divorce, and extending a guarantee of alimony to both men and women.[88] Although Bolshevik interventions on behalf of women had only just begun by the time Doty and the others left, they would gain attention from all over the world, especially from modern "new women" in the United States.[89]

In addition to a more extensive discussion of women and "women's issues," Bryant's book also includes a chapter on Russian children, who would be another significant draw for American women in coming years: Bryant describes Russian children's sweet temperament, their cooperative instincts, the Bolshevik efforts to institute "self-government" in schools, and Russian children's dire need for material aid. Significant numbers of American women would travel to Russia as relief workers to help Russian children, especially during the 1921 famine and its aftermath; others came as social workers, educators, and journalists, eager to witness Soviet attempts to create the "new person."[90]

Doty does acknowledge women's efforts to secure the vote in Russia immediately following the fall of the tsar, and notes women's visibility in all areas of Russian society. Early in her narrative, discussing the train ride across Siberia that took her to St. Petersburg, Doty notes that "the Siberian women, like the men, were strong, rough creatures. They wore rubber boots and short skirts and had shawls tied about their heads. The younger women had the beauty of health and strength. They worked in the fields with men, their labor was the equal of theirs."[91] She describes Russian women as men's "comrades and equals," and also remarks upon a Siberian woman traveling on the same train with her as representative of the women of her village "to demand that clothing be sent to her town in exchange for the foodstuff being sent to Petrograd." This woman, through Doty's telling, offered at once a haunting portrait of the dangers women faced as well as an inspiring tale of their strength, solidarity, and resilience: "She was full of tales of her village. Two deserting soldiers had just visited her town and raped a young girl. The women had risen up in wrath and beaten

---

[88] Wendy Z. Goldman, *Women, the State, and Revolution: Soviet Family Policy & Social Life, 1917–1936* (Cambridge: Cambridge University Press, 1995), 51.

[89] Mickenberg, *American Girls in Red Russia*.

[90] Bryant, *Six Red Months in Russia*, 251–58.

[91] Doty, *Behind the Battle Line*, 36.

the men and thrust them out." Doty concludes, "It was a crude, elemental world, full of hot passion, into which I was rushing."[92]

Books by both Bryant and Beatty include a chapter on the Women's Battalion of Death, organized by Maria Bochkareva, a veteran of Russian military service. With an intense desire to fight for her country, and in response to flagging morale and increasing desertions among Russian military men, Bochkareva had organized an all-woman regiment to shame the men into continuing their fight. Her battalion was called to defend the Provisional Government at the Winter Palace during the Bolshevik coup, but they were quickly overpowered. Doty apparently interviewed Bochkareva during a tour she took of the United States in 1918 but did not include the article she subsequently published, "Women Who Would A-Soldiering Go," in her book. Doty clearly was deeply uncomfortable with the idea of women on the battlefield and because her interview with Bochkareva occurred in the United States, may have decided it did not fit the parameters of her book. Beatty, in contrast, suggested in her chapter on the battalion that women's military service proved their strength and fitness for voting. Bryant spent much of her chapter on the battalion trying to prove that the women had been duped into supporting the Provisional Government, and were now mainly in support of the Bolsheviks.

Behind Behind the Battle Line

It is in some ways surprising to find only one chapter on Russian women in Doty's book, given her ostensible focus on women. The chapters on countries other than Russia, which have not been included in this edition, do focus on women: Chapter 1, "Autocratic Japan," was subtitled "The Woman Slave"; Chapter 2, "Awakening China," was subtitled "The Bound Woman"; Chapter 10 was called "Swedish Women—The Genius" (although in the table of contents it is entitled "Materialistic Sweden"); Chapter 11, "Vital Norway," was subtitled "The Woman Pioneer." While the chapters on France and England—"Inspiring France" and "Warriors of the Spirit: Democratic England," respectively—do not have women in their titles, their focus is upon women as well, and the "warriors of the spirit" in England are, in fact, women. Still, *Behind the Battle Line*, with seven chapters on Russia and only one chapter on each of the other countries Doty visited, contains as much material about women in Russia as it does about women elsewhere. This difference in focus is another reason the Russia discussion seems best read apart from the other chapters in *Behind the Battle Line*.

Beyond the challenges posed by the fact that the Russian chapters of *Behind the Battle Line* were not intended for publication on their own is the fact that Doty published similar accounts in multiple venues. All originally appeared, with slight varia-

---

[92] Ibid.

tions, in periodicals and newspapers, including *Good Housekeeping*, the *New-York Tribune* (which syndicated some of her pieces), *The Atlantic*, and *The Nation*, a British weekly. Reading all of these accounts gives a fuller portrait of her experiences, but because they contain a great deal of the same material, including all of these pieces would be repetitive. For the sake of coherence this edition uses the text published in *Behind the Battle Line*, but when there are significant differences between the version published there and elsewhere, it is noted in the footnotes. This edition incorporates relevant parts of the introduction and conclusion to *Behind the Battle Line* and some material from Chapter 1 (here retitled "Crossing the Pacific" from the original "Autocratic Japan" to reflect that only material marking Doty's travels has been included). Also included are selections from Chapters 10–14 (collectively titled "Heading Home" in this edition) in order to give a sense of Doty's journey from and back to the United States, and specifically into and out of Russia amidst the challenges posed by wartime. Inclusion of Doty's travel to and from Russia reflects conventions of other narratives.[93] In editing this text for publication, I have tried to maintain a balance between preserving Doty's original language (e.g., keeping her use of "czar," though "tsar" is more typically used today) and making changes to reflect proper or more contemporary spelling and usage and to maintain consistency through the text. Ellipses indicate where material has been cut from the original versions. I have taken some liberties with the illustrations, adding, for instance, an image of Doty and Florence Harding on the boat to Japan and Russia and an illustration from material Doty published in *Good Housekeeping*, and leaving out some images from the Russian part of *Behind the Battle Line* that felt less essential to Doty's narrative (such as additional pictures of her permits to enter various buildings).

Doty's experiences and observations about women in other countries remind us that the Russian Revolution cannot be considered apart from the World War in which it appeared or the feminist transformations that were affecting all parts of the world—despite the fact that Doty did not emphasize the latter in her discussion of Russia, with other circumstances too pressing to ignore. Indeed, *Behind the Battle Line* opens with a preface that gives little indication of Russia's dominance in the book itself, framing the revolutionary events in the context of stages of world development:

> In Japan, for instance, women are openly sold into industry and prostitution, and a God sent emperor sits upon the throne. In that land to be a member of the Y.W.C.A. was to be a rebel and a revolutionist. Japan socially is in the Middle Ages. When I reached Russia on the other hand I found that the working people had seized the government and that Maxim Gorky was in danger of imprisonment as a conservative. I had leaped forward into the Twenty-first Century.

---

[93] Both Beatty and Bryant recount the circumstances of their travels to and from Russia.

Importantly, although Doty places Bolshevik Russia ahead of several other countries in terms of development, she is careful to condemn the violent methods by which they had arrived at this point. In that sense, though still nominally ruled by a king—and this only in the "twentieth" rather than the "twenty-first century"—Doty suggests that England has achieved an ideal balance of orderly, democratic development: "In England the people are slowly taking possession of their own," she asserts. They were doing so "not as in Russia by the force of the bayonet, but through universal education and the intellectual intelligence of the masses."[94]

Although left out of the text itself in this edition, Doty's portrait of her friend Emmeline Pethick-Lawrence—to whom *Behind the Battle Line* was dedicated (the book's front matter contains a full-page photograph of Pethick-Lawrence, and the dedication, "To Emmeline Pethick-Lawrence," adds, "who has made my dream of great women a reality")—is worth quoting at length, for it suggests the way in which Doty herself envisioned societies ideally evolving not simply to include more women, but in fact fundamentally remade along lines inspired by women's activism. Doty met peace activist and suffragist Emmeline Pethick-Lawrence as part of her 1915 journey to The Hague with the Women's Peace Party. The two women remained friends for life; Doty admired Pethick-Lawrence's commitment to social justice as well as her companionate marriage to Frederick Lawrence (after the two married they shared the combined last name of Pethick-Lawrence). The wealthy couple's homes in London and Surrey would become sites of refuge and comfort for Doty over the years. In her chapter of *Behind the Battle Line* on England, Doty notes:

> The two names that will go down in history as the famous leaders of the militant movement are Emmeline Pankhurst and Emmeline Pethick-Lawrence. But Mrs. Pankhurst was the body, Mrs. Lawrence the spirit. When the militants took to smashing store windows and burning houses Mrs. Lawrence protested. She would give her life for the cause, but she would not hurt others. Her way of winning was through the spirit. It was the woman's way. She left the organization. Today she continues true to those ideals. Her method of service in the great world struggle is through the spirit. She urges women to be warriors of the spirit. She goes back and forth through the land speaking. I heard her many times and wherever she went hearts were unlocked and leapt to meet hers, and there came a great determination to die if need be for the race to come. This is the gist of what she said:
>
> "Along with the physical battle that engulfs the world, goes a gigantic spiritual struggle, and day by day that spiritual battle wins new victories. We see it in the enfranchisement of women, in the fight for Mothers' Pensions, in President Wilson's speeches, in the democratic peace terms, in the

---

[94] Doty, *Behind the Battle Line*, vii–viii.

overthrowing of the Czar in Russia. These are victories that can never be lost. Whichever army advances on the field of battle the fight for freedom will be won. The spirit arises triumphant. Come, join this army of the spirit. Be a soldier of life." ...

Such is the battle the women wage. They seek to create a new and better world, a world in which each new life will be born unfettered.[95]

As is evident in the wider resonance of this portrait, Doty's own feminist activism and her ardent commitment to peace have to be seen as influencing the book as a whole, a book that is in a sense complicated by the fact that Doty happened to find herself in the midst of the Bolshevik Revolution. As she concluded at the end of her chapter on England:

> In the years to come when the war is over, women of every land must meet together. In great international groups they must discuss the problems of mothers and babies, and when these women return to their homes they must live and fight for these plans and dreams, and then at the end of a year or two years return again to recount triumphs and failures. Until finally through the inspiration of organized motherhood—each baby that opens its eyes will open them to a world rid of war and to a life of freedom and love.

Doty did not find such a world in revolutionary Russia, but she appreciated the opportunity to witness efforts to remake a society, and undoubtedly the experience gave her hope that the wider world might one day be remade along more just and humane lines.

Suggested Further Reading

Acton, Edward, Vladimir Cherniaev, and William G. Rosenberg. *Critical Companion to the Russian Revolution, 1914–1921*. Bloomington: Indiana University Press, 1997.

Alonso, Harriet Hyman. *Peace as a Women's Issue: A History of the U.S. Movement for World Peace and Women's Rights*. Syracuse, NY: Syracuse University Press, 1993.

Beatty, Bessie. *The Red Heart of Russia*. New York: Century, 1919.

Bryant, Louise. *Six Red Months in Russia*. New York: George H. Doran, 1918.

Chatterjee, Choi. "'Odds and Ends of the Russian Revolution, 1917–1920': Gender and American Travel Narratives. *Journal of Women's History* 20, no. 4 (Winter 2008): 10–33.

---

[95] Ibid., 186–87; 189–90.

Doty, Madeleine Z. *One Woman Determined to Make a Difference: The Life of Madeleine Zabriskie Doty.* Edited by Alice Duffy Rhinehart. Bethlehem, PA: Lehigh University Press, 2001.

Dumenil, Lynn. *The Second Line of Defense: American Women and World War I.* Chapel Hill: University of North Carolina Press, 2017.

Fitzpatrick, Sheila. *The Russian Revolution.* 3rd ed. New York: Oxford University Press, 2008.

Lutes, Jean Marie. *Front Page Girls: Women Journalists in American Culture and Fiction, 1880–1930.* Ithaca, NY: Cornell University Press, 2006.

Mickenberg, Julia L. *American Girls in Red Russia: Chasing the Soviet Dream.* Chicago: University of Chicago Press, 2017.

Pipes, Richard. *A Concise History of the Russian Revolution.* New York: Alfred A. Knopf, 1995.

Rabinowitch, Alexander. *The Bolsheviks in Power: The First Year of Soviet Rule in Petrograd.* Bloomington: Indiana University Press, 2007.

Ruthchild, Rochelle Goldberg. *Equality & Revolution: Women's Rights in the Russian Empire, 1905–1917.* Pittsburgh: University of Pittsburgh Press, 2010.

Stockdale, Melissa K. "'My Death for the Motherland Is Happiness': Women, Patriotism, and Soldiering in Russia's Great War, 1914–1917." *American Historical Review* 109, no. 1 (2004): 78–116.

Wheeler-Bennett, John W. *Brest-Litovsk: The Forgotten Peace, March 1918.* New York: W. W. Norton, 1938.

BEHIND THE BATTLE LINE
AROUND THE WORLD IN 1918

BY

MADELEINE Z. DOTY

ILLUSTRATED

NEW YORK

THE MACMILLAN COMPANY

1918

All rights reserved

TO

EMMELINE PETHICK-LAWRENCE

WHO HAS MADE MY DREAM OF GREAT
WOMEN A REALITY

PREFACE

There is a great fascination about warring Europe. Across the seas a world drama is being enacted. One cannot keep away. Each year the scene changes. Having seen the first act one must see the next. The call came to me. I had been to Europe twice since the war. This was the third trip.[1] This time I was to go around the world.

I knew that parallel with the physical battle that engulfs us, runs a great spiritual struggle. That was the drama I was watching. I tried to discover the dreams and plans of the women of the future,[2] what the folks at home strove for, where the spiritual drama led. In each country I sought the heart of things. I made no attempt to acquire facts and figures. In superficial details this book undoubtedly has inaccuracies. It is merely a bird's-eye view of a mixed up world, with a glimpse of the new spiritual order which arises out of the muddle.

A very important factor in the consideration of world affairs is the different stage of development of the different nations. To treat of matters internationally when one nation is in the Middle Ages and another in the Twenty-first Century is almost impossible. In Japan, for instance, women are openly sold into industry and prostitution, and a God sent emperor sits upon the throne. In that land to be a member of the YWCA was to be a rebel and a revolutionist.[3] Japan socially is in the Middle Ages.

When I reached Russia on the other hand I found that the working people had seized the government and that Maxim Gorky was in danger of imprisonment as a

---

[1] As recorded in her book *Short Rations*, Doty traveled to The Hague in 1915 with a group of about seventy women for an international women's peace gathering, and from there visited Germany, England, and France, and then returned to Europe a second time specifically to study conditions in Germany.

[2] This terminology was popular at the time, signaling "modern" as in Isadora Duncan's paean to the "dancer of the future" or rhetoric about the "new woman," the "new negro," the "new psychology," the "new education," etc.

[3] Founded in 1855, the Young Women's Christian Association is an international organization with affiliates across the United States. It grew out of a rise in Evangelical Protestantism in the early to mid-nineteenth century. Rather than simply a recreational or social club with a Christian orientation, at its height in the first decades of the twentieth century, the YWCA was an activist organization, working toward desegregation, labor legislation, and social welfare.

conservative.[4] I had leaped forward into the Twenty-first Century.... But this uneven state of world development will not long continue. In every country exists a group of people spiritually awake. They are fighting the fight for the new freedom.[5] In a generation the backward nations will achieve the struggles of centuries and be brought up to a Twentieth Century standard of democracy.[6] Travel, moving picture shows, the mingling of races, the exchange of literature will bring new light everywhere. Fifty years from today kings will have vanished and Parliaments and Congresses be the governing force in each nation. With the dawn of such a day wars will cease and a true internationalism be established. And in this new order which arises women are destined to play a large part. For in those countries which are most advanced women are most active....

[Looking toward the future], before my eyes grew a dazzling vision of an army of mothers joining hands the world around, battling for the rights of the world's children, creating a new and better race of men and women, bringing to fruition the kingdom of God upon earth.

---

[4] See ch. 4, n. 6.

[5] See n. 1.

[6] Ideas about a hierarchy of races and nations were very common in the early twentieth century.

Chapter I

CROSSING THE PACIFIC

The big steamer swung out from the dock at Vancouver. A drizzly rain concealed the beauty of the harbor. My eyes clung to the shore. It was my last glimpse of America. Ahead lay a big adventure.

The ship was crowded. There were three persons in every cabin. People for Russia, India, China, and Japan were streaming across the Pacific. It was the only safe way. Yet even the Pacific has reminders of war. A coat of gray war-paint covers the steamer, making it look like a monster cruiser. But gay music floats from the saloon. A Filipino band is playing a two-step. The passengers are chatting gayly. As we steam down the harbor we take stock of one another. For ten days we must live together.

I find as roommates a Norwegian missionary and the wife of a member of the British Legation in Peking. The missionaries are numerous; they number seventy-two. The steamship people have used them as Bibles, and put one in every cabin. The other passengers are buyers, bankers, merchants, and government officials. It isn't a mixable company. Upstairs in the saloon the missionaries gather about the piano and sing hymns. On the deck below fox-trots and bunny-hugs are in progress. But the ocean is a great leveler. During the first night we encounter a mountainous sea. In the morning, missionary and merchant lean over the deck-rail in mutual agony. Souls may differ, but stomachs are of one brotherhood.

But the Pacific is not long angry. Unlike the Atlantic, a few hours transform it. The turbulent surface becomes as smooth as a mill-pond. There are days of glowing sunshine. As we steam north the air nips and bites. We scurry from the sunny spots on deck to the tea-room. In the long uneventful hours acquaintance ripens into friendship...

The journey nears its end—twenty-four hours more and it will be over. But even as we sigh with content, little black clouds appear in the sky. The wireless tells of two typhoons raging off the China coast. Spurts of rain and gusts of wind beat against the ship. Again we toss and moan. We have caught the edge of a storm. But in the evening the clouds break. Far off on the horizon, in a golden sunset, we see the dark blue hills of Japan. The Japanese hurry to the deck. A light breaks through their stolid faces.

That night it is hard to sleep. To-morrow we enter the Land of the Rising Sun.

When I awake in the morning we are already entering the harbor of Yokohama. I climb onto the berth and poke my head out of the port-hole. Drops of rain fall on my face. I see long, low, wooden docks, and European buildings old and dilapidated. We might be arriving in Hoboken or some equally ugly American port.

I fight down my disappointment. Fortunately there is no time for thought—all is hurry and bustle of departure.

My cabin-mate, the wife of the member of the British Legation, and I decide to travel together. She has lived much in the East and was born in China. To her the strange customs of the Orient are familiar.

Figure 3. Doty with Florence Harding, wife of the member of British Legation, on deck of steamer to Japan and Russia, 1917. Madeleine Z. Doty Papers, Sophia Smith Collection, Smith College (Northampton, MA).

For two days we journeyed through the land. Our train slid past the Inland Sea—that stretch of vivid blue water, whose shoreline is studded with shapely mountains possessing a beauty almost unnatural. It is an idealized version of beautiful Lake Geneva for mile after mile, until the eye grows weary with such continuous exquisite loveliness.

After a night of tossing, the small Japanese boat landed us on the Corean shore. Gone was the miniature loveliness, the superficial cleanliness, the smooth running life of Japan. The Corean peninsula is a stretch of flat, sandy waste with mountainous ridges, the little town Fusan, at which we landed, unspeakably dirty, the buildings crude and ugly.

It took two days and a night to travel through the sandy wastes and mud huts of Corea. The climate was dry and arid, like our far West. There are few trees.

After we reached Mukden we passed into Chinese territory.... For a day and a night we joggled and bounced over a bad roadbed in our shabby Chinese train. At night a bundle of bedclothes was tossed in and we spread these on the slippery sofas. There were no regular sleeping cars. At ten in the morning we pulled into Peking. My first impression was one of keen disappointment. As I passed under the great wall I stepped into paved streets with European buildings and high walls. No wonder the Chinese fear Europeans. The first mile of their city belongs to foreign embassies. I stayed at the British Embassy. It was indeed lovely, with its smooth lawns and green trees and low buildings. Like a bit of England dumped down into a high-walled enclosure with Hindu soldiers at every gate. But I had a sense of resentment, a feeling that I was being shut away from the East. I kept asking, "Where is China?" It was not until the second day that I discovered the real Peking. Out beyond the Embassy I journeyed in a rickshaw. We turned into a long avenue that leads to the Forbidden City and the Palace of the Former Emperors. The high wall shut out the palace buildings. But the tiled yellow roofs rose above the wall. They glistened in the sunlight like bits of the sun itself. The impressive gateways were buildings and their dashes of red, blue and yellow tiling lent color and character to everything.

We passed under the great wall through the gateway that separated the palace from the real Peking. Here at last was China. Such life, such activity.

Chapter II
ACROSS SIBERIA DURING THE BOLSHEVIK REVOLUTION

I left Peking in the evening. Shrill Chinese chatter penetrated every corner of the train. The next day the walled towns with their narrow alleys disappeared; the hills vanished, the land flattened, mud huts filled the horizon. At Mukden we encountered again the Japanese. There came a night on a Japanese train. It was a train de luxe, an advertisement on the part of Japan of her competence, a sort of "See how good it is to be ruled by us!"[1] I had a compartment to myself and a real bed with dazzling white linen sheets. But this ride was brief. In the morning we arrived at a small frontier town and boarded a dingy, dirty, Russian train. Despite the dirt I felt out of the East, back in the West.[2] The Russian language is as unintelligible as the Chinese, but it has a familiar note, just as the rough log houses in place of mud and stone huts, and the long, belted, fur-lined coat and fur cap instead of the pigtail and shirt, bring one back with a rush from queer customs and mysticism to a crude but modern civilization.

At seven in the evening we reached Harbin and Siberia. Here I was to catch the Vladivostok express for Petrograd. The temperature had dropped 30 degrees; it was dark and cold as I stepped into the large waiting-room. The warmth of the place was grateful, but the relief was momentary, the air was foul. Sprawled over the floor, on the benches, in the chairs, were hundreds of Russian refugees.[3]

There wasn't an unoccupied floor spot. Women and babies lay flat upon their backs with their bags as head-rests. Dirty Russian soldiers sat upon curled-up legs and smoked and spat upon the floor, and littered the place with cigarette butts.

---

[1] Japan occupied most maritime regions of Siberia following the Russo-Japanese War in 1905; although Japan had also gained control of the Chinese city of Mukden in the war, by 1911 Chinese warlords had gained power over the city. In 1914 the city was officially renamed Shenyang (its name from ancient China), but people often still referred to it as Mukden.

[2] This comment is noteworthy because Russia's liminal status between East and West has been a matter of controversy and discussion. Americans tended to imagine Russians as backward and Asiatic (rather than European) and prone to despotism. Hence the phrase "darkest Russia," which came into popular usage in the United States in the mid- to late nineteenth century.

[3] The war created an acute refugee crisis—and a related health and housing crisis—as men, women, and children who were driven from their homes by advancing German armies disembarked from freight cars in which they had escaped and were then unable to travel any further.

Rough-looking Cossacks with unshaven faces, armed and knived, pushed their way in and out of the crowded room. The Russian revolution had descended upon me. I shrank back frightened. All around me was a babble of voices, but not one word could I understand. It was seven, and I had had no food since one o'clock.

In the far end of the room was a refreshment counter, but the crowd was too dense to reach it. I searched for a place to sit, but there was none to be had even on the floor. I stood on one foot and then on the other. Two hours crawled by. The bulletin board showed the Petrograd train was many hours late. I could endure the discomfort no longer. I struggled to the door.

It was dangerous to leave the station. Stories had reached me in China of the disorder in Harbin. There had been shooting in the streets, and hardly a day passed without some killing. Chinese, Russians, and Japanese filled the town, no one was in control, the foreign consulates remained under cover.[4] But bad air, hunger, and fatigue drove me forth. Instinct said the Chinaman was to be trusted.[5] I hailed a rickshaw and climbed in. There is one word common to all lands. "Hotel," I said. We slipped out into the dark night. Soon I was at Harbin's one hotel. That place, like the station, bulged with humanity. Beds filled the corridors. Russia was spewing forth an endless stream. Even here my English tongue brought no response till a young man in European dress stepped forward. I had asked for the British Consulate. "Let me take you there," he said. "I have an automobile." Trust is a prime requisite for travel in warring Europe. I gladly accepted. A quick, breathless ride in the winter night set me before the house of the English Consul. But my reception by the young consular assistant was not cordial. Life was difficult and dangerous, strange women an added responsibility, my supperless condition a vexation, for the young man had nothing to offer. We chatted for a couple of hours. At eleven my companion insisted on seeing me to my train. We deserted the sidewalk and took to the snow-covered road.

"It is safer," said my companion, "for there has been much shooting lately."

It was a mile to the station. The night air bit, and my feet grew numb. When we arrived we learned to our dismay the train was still hours late. It wouldn't arrive before two A. M. I was faint from hunger. I clamored for food. Reluctantly my companion set out with me for the hotel. A hard piece of bread, a stale egg, and a weak cup of

---

[4] The February Revolution had an almost immediate impact on the city of Harbin, which is at one end of the Trans-Siberian Railroad. In the summer of 1917, a power triangle began to emerge between competing interests, including the railway (in Harbin, controlled by the Chinese Eastern Railway or CER), Chinese military forces, and railway workers, who tended to be pro-Bolshevik. In the fall, wealthy Russians began to move to Harbin from Russia, while left-wing émigré Russians made stopovers in Harbin on their way back into the country, making the city a key point of conflict.

[5] Earlier in the narrative, in material that has been cut from this edition, Doty talks about the democratic spirit of the Chinese (as opposed to the Japanese) and of feeling more comfortable in China than in Japan or Korea.

tea gave me back a little courage. I begged my companion to go home and to bed. But his sporting blood was up. He insisted on seeing the thing through. We returned to the station. We crowded into the packed building and found standing room near the door. One o'clock came and went. Rough-looking Russian soldiers gazed suspiciously at the neat khaki-clad Englishman beside me and brushed rudely against him. He swung his cane nonchalantly and looked uneasily about. Minute after minute crept by. Two o'clock came, then two-thirty and the shrill whistle of a train.

I bade my companion good-by and staggered up the steps of a first-class state car. Would my berth reservation be correct? A thick-set man in a Russian blouse unlocked a stateroom door. I was too tired to notice my surroundings. The grimy dirt of the floor, the gray sheets went unheeded. My heart rejoiced at the unoccupied upper berth. I flung off my clothes and dropped into the lower berth. The seclusion and rest were heavenly, but a wave of loneliness swept over me. Was there any one on the train who spoke English? Had the members of the Y.M.C.A. or the American correspondent whom I expected caught this train?[6] Should I find them in a neighboring car? Then I smiled. I remembered the letter an editor of a magazine had given me. It was a letter "To whom it may concern." It was the last sentence in the letter which made me chuckle. It said, "We can vouch for the character of the bearer of this note and will be responsible for her actions and conduct throughout her journey." Poor editor! To vouch for a stray woman in turbulent Russia! I chuckled again and dropped asleep.

It was six A. M. when I awoke with a start. My stateroom door had been flung open. The Russian porter was showing a Cossack soldier into my compartment. I sat up in my berth and let forth a flood of English; I gesticulated wildly, but the Russians only shook their heads. Then the Cossack dismissed the porter, closed the door, and locked it. Tales of Cossack brutality surged through my mind. I felt for my money under my pillow. My heart beat violently. The soldier was distinctly disagreeable. He saw my discomfiture and enjoyed it. He gathered up my scattered garments and flung them into my berth. Then he slowly took off his coat and shoes and climbed into the

---

[6] Doty's significant contact with members of the YMCA points to the organization's influence in Russia during the revolution and Civil War. YMCA representatives had been in Russia since 1900, when a club, the *Mayak* ("lighthouse" in Russian), was opened in St. Petersburg. This effort was part of a wider international missionary agenda espoused by the YMCA, which worked to spread American and Western-style ideas of Christian enlightenment. Russian strictures on the club were lessened after the February Revolution, allowing for expansion of the organization. American support for the Provisional Government and desire to keep it in place had a significant impact on Wilson's decision to enter the war. By the summer of 1917, following a failed Bolshevik coup known as the "July Days," which aimed to capitalize on war weariness and low morale among Russian soldiers, the YMCA stepped up its work with Russian soldiers in order to increase morale and bolster Russian war efforts. A new wave of YMCA representatives arrived in Russia in October and November, coincident with the onset of the Bolshevik Revolution—hence their presence alongside Doty, who was arriving at the same moment.

upper berth. I heard him making his preparations for sleep. I listened breathlessly till all was still. Then I stealthily began to put on my clothes. When dressed in my coat and skirt I crawled out of the lower berth and stood up. The soldier was lying above me with eyes wide open.

He had a cigarette between his lips. He puffed at it leisurely and grinned at me amusedly. A wave of resentment seized me, but I picked up my comb and brush and began quickly to do up my hair. My hand trembled. Then suddenly I remembered the editor's letter, "We will be responsible for her actions and conduct throughout her journey." My lips twitched; laughter surged up. My strained nerves relaxed, and fear vanished. I gathered up my possessions, unbolted the door, flung it open, and in a moment was out in the corridor. But it was dark night outside. Not until nine A. M. would light appear on the horizon. Every compartment door was closed and locked. At the end of the car the porter snored peacefully in his bunk. I stood in the swaying train corridor and waited for dawn. My courage oozed. I wanted to turn and run home.

Figure 4. Illustration originally accompanying Doty's article "How I Came to Petrograd," in *Good Housekeeping*, July 1918, 42.

At last day came. At ten the doors began to open. I wandered up and down, inquiring, "Do you speak English?" and "Parlez-vous francais?" At last I found a Russian who spoke French.

"Is there an English-speaking person on the train?" I asked. "Yes," he said, "there are two American boys in the rear car."

Joyfully I hurried back and timidly knocked on their door. In a moment a sleepy American boy stuck his head out at me. I explained my predicament.

"Don't you worry," was the cheery answer.

"We'll be dressed in a minute." And presently two boys from New York City and a Serbian soldier who spoke English fluently were listening to my story.

It was the Serbian soldier who took command. "We three are traveling together for an American firm," he said. "We have two compartments between us. There is an unoccupied berth in mine. You'd better come travel with us." Gladly I consented, and soon my luggage was beside the Serbian's.[7]

When I had washed, we went to the dining-car. There were a few Russian women on the train, but they knew no English. The Y.M.C.A. men and the American correspondent had not turned up. The passengers were Russian merchants, army officers, and soldiers. I fought hard to keep up my courage. The American boys were shy and inexperienced. Petrograd seemed a long way off. Twelve more days and nights of travel—an eternity! It was the Serbian soldier to whom I turned. He was young, only twenty-five. He had black hair and burning black eyes, a pale face full of restless energy. He had been in the Serbian Army since 1912, and in the great retreat. His nerves were spent and jangling. Wounded and nerve-racked, he had been discharged. For a year he had been in America. His friends called him Nick, and I soon followed suit. Nick could speak Russian like a native. From him we learned that my adventures of the night were the subject of conversation. I did not receive much sympathy. To the Russians I seemed finicky. Life had gotten down to the elementals. There was no room for conventions. For a woman to object to sharing a compartment with a man was fussiness.[8] The lady had better stay at home if she is that particular. I swallowed hard and tried to adjust myself to new standards. I strove to drop into the fighting man's world of crudeness, blows, and danger. I could see that even Nick thought me sensitive.

It was a queer, rushing world into which I had come. Even that first day there were wild stories afloat—that Kerensky had fallen; that he had not fallen but was in

---

[7] It seems notable that Doty is immediately willing to trust these three men (but not the Cossack) apparently just because of their language, dress, and manners.

[8] American visitors to Russia frequently commented on the fact of having to share train compartments with the opposite sex: many were made uncomfortable by the practice, but some reveled in what appeared as evidence that Russians had fewer sexual inhibitions than Americans.

possession of Petrograd and fighting rebellion.[9] Smoke and talk filled the train. Cigarette butts and ashes covered the floor. The air grew fouler and fouler. People sneezed and coughed, but no one opened a window. There is a prejudice against fresh air in Siberia and Russia. Many of the car windows are nailed down, and not once during the journey was there an attempt at ventilation. At night the air grew cold and rank, in the day hot and fetid. Over and over our lungs breathed this foulness. My throat grew sore; I began to cough. The station stops were a godsend. Flinging on our coats we marched back and forth on the platform. At each stop the entire train turned out. Every man was armed with a tea-kettle. At the stations were huge samovars or big tanks of boiling water. The tea-kettles quickly filled, back rushed the passengers. Then from every compartment floated the odor of tea, the smell of cigarettes, and the babble of voices.

All day and most of the night this went on. When the evening of the first day came I was half sick and utterly weary. The Serbian soldier sensed my fatigue. An understanding light came into his eyes. He began to tell me about his mother and sister. They had been taken prisoners by the Germans. An occasional postcard at intervals of three months was his only news. His heart was torn with anxiety. "You know," he said, "a Serbian places his sister before all others; he stands by her through everything. He never marries until she marries, and he cares for her always." He showed me some presents—lovely silks from Japan—which he was hoarding to take to his mother and sister on the day when he could go to them. But it wasn't homesickness made Nick tell me of his family. It was his way of making me one of them. When he had finished, he said, " We fellows have decided to bunk in together, or rather one of us will share your stateroom with the soldier, and you can have this place to yourself." A lump came up in my throat. Here was a fighting man, who had killed many, still capable of infinite tenderness. It was with a very thankful heart I locked my stateroom door and delighted in the blessed seclusion.

---

[9] Alexander Kerensky, a socialist lawyer, was part of the original cabinet established as part of the Provisional Government, which took power after the tsar was deposed in March 1917 (February on the Russian, or Julian, calendar). Originally, he served as a liaison between liberals, who dominated the Provisional Government, and socialist intellectuals, mainly Mensheviks (the more moderate wing of the Social Democrats or Marxists) and Socialist Revolutionaries, or SRs, who dominated the Executive Committee of the Petrograd Soviet, which vied for power with the Provisional Government. Kerensky became the Provisional Government's minister of war, and, after the July Days, effectively became leader of the Provisional Government. He was also vice chairman of the Petrograd Soviet. Despite this important role, he lacked a real political base and enjoyed very little trust or respect. Kerensky's standing was eroded further by an attempted coup from the Right in August led by General Lavr Kornilov. When the Bolsheviks, led by Vladimir Lenin, seized upon the growing distrust of the Provisional Government amongst workers and soldiers and orchestrated a coup on October 25 (November 6), Kerensky was in no position to oppose it; and when the Winter Palace, the seat of the Provisional Government, fell on the night of October 25, Kerensky slipped out a side entrance and fled the city.

In the morning I woke with splitting head and aching throat. I could scarcely breathe. When Nick appeared I begged for air. He wrestled with the window and managed to open it a little. But the respite was brief. The porter on our train was an ugly youth, a Social Democrat of the extreme Left, a Bolshevik. To him we were all hateful, capitalists and bourgeois. I knew no Russian words with which to make friends. I had not learned to say Tavarish—comrade. He discovered the open window and slammed it to with a torrent of angry words.

I struggled through the day. At each station we hurried to the platform to learn the news. Conflicting stories poured over the wires. Now it was that there was rioting and bloodshed in Petrograd and Moscow, that the Bolsheviki were in the ascendant. Again that Kerensky had moved on Petrograd with an army and quelled the uprising. When the news for the Bolsheviki was bad our surly young porter grew more and more ugly. He took my drinking glass from me; then he removed my electric light. I began to fear him and sat with my door locked. I had difficulty in keeping Nick from smashing the boy's head.

All the time our train moved steadily forward, and to my amazement I discovered that Siberia was beautiful. There were hills, and great woods, and rushing rivers. Though it was November, many places were without snow. When we drew near Irkutsk, there were snow-covered mountains and a great lake. Siberia had much of the grandeur of Canada. But the villages were crude, the houses chiefly log huts.

The peasant huts have but two rooms. Sometimes as many as twelve people sleep in one room.

The Siberian women, like the men, were strong, rough creatures. They wore rubber boots and short skirts and had shawls tied about their heads. The younger women had the beauty of health and strength. They worked in the fields with men, their labor was the equal of theirs. Sex differences were not considered. There was no woman's question. The men and women were comrades and equals. At one station a Siberian woman boarded our train for Petrograd. She went as the representative of the women of her village to demand that clothing be sent to her town in exchange for the foodstuff being sent to Petrograd. She was full of tales of her village. Two deserting soldiers had just visited her town and raped a young girl. The women had risen up in wrath and beaten the men and thrust them out.[10] It was a crude, elemental world, full of hot passion, into which I was rushing.

As the days went on my cold grew worse, until finally I could only lie in my berth. Through the long, weary hours Nick talked and nursed me. When my cold threatened to go on my lungs, he hunted up a young Russian soldier who was a medical student. They sat beside me and discussed my needs. I began to be quite outside myself,

---

[10] This observation on Doty's part is evidence of women's new assertiveness and engagement in civic life. Prior to the revolution, peasant women were routinely abused by their husbands and by other men in their communities. The revolution brought immediate legal changes for women but also a new consciousness.

like a third person watching a story unfold. I saw a sick woman and a Serbian soldier rushing on into a great maelstrom. His nerves tightened and his body strengthened at this new responsibility which had been placed upon him.

Heroic measures were adopted by my young doctors. It was the method of the trenches and soldiers. I was to sweat my cold out. Army coats were piled on top of me, my window closed tight. At the stations Nick bought bottles of boiled milk.

This he sternly poured down my throat. Minute by minute my discomfort increased. My body ached; sweat poured from me. But Nick relentlessly stood guard. Then he began to tell me stories—the tragedies of battle. Nearly all his friends had been killed, his best friend before his eyes. A shell severed the head from the body. That friend's body was dear to Nick. Between the bursting bombs he crawled out to the battlefield. Tenderly he gathered up that headless form and bore it back to the trenches. Blood from his friend's wounds infected open cuts in Nick's hands. For weeks he tossed in high fever. But the infected hands and arms were not amputated, and in time he recovered. As I listened to these tales my own suffering seemed small, the endurance of men enormous. Feebly my hand rose to my forehead in salute.

The next morning I was weak, but my cold had broken. Now the stories we heard at the stations grew alarming. It was evident a great revolution had taken place in Petrograd. Still our train rushed on. But the stops grew tense with excitement.

Men huddled together and felt for their pistols. The car doors were locked. This express train with its first-class carriages and sleeping compartments was a sign of the plutocracy that had been. Any moment we might expect to have the windows smashed. Nick tried to keep the news from me, but the American boys came with their stories. I ceased to be afraid. One could not think in terms of the individual, life was moving too fast. But sick fear had crept into the hearts of the Russian merchants. They stormed and raged.

One mean little Russian repudiated his country. "All Russians are cattle," he said. "They ought to be milked and then killed."[11]

Nick came to me white with rage. "That man must be beaten." I held on to his hands and tried to quiet him. "Well," he fumed, "I won't hit him, but next station I'll put him out on the platform and tell the crowd what he said. They'll tear him limb from limb."

"It isn't the way, Nick," I begged, "it isn't the way." Gradually his anger subsided.

"You see," he said, "I'm not good. I'm a brute. I've told you I was." But in the end it was words and not blows that were used with the Russian merchant. What was said I never knew, but thereafter the man walked with bowed head and cringing step.

And now the last day of the trip had come. Russian soldiers had begun to crowd on the train. They slept in the corridors or standing in passageways. But there was no

---

[11] In both *The Nation* and *Good Housekeeping*, Doty refers to the man as a "mean little Jew." It is not clear why she made the change in her book.

violence. At some of the stations there had been rioting. Windows had been smashed and houses burned. But no move was made against the train, and at six one morning we pulled quietly into Petrograd. There was a great stillness over the station. There were no hurrying porters or calling cabmen, none of the bustle of arrival. We filed silently out into the street. It was like the dead of night. A few people lurked in doorways, but the big snow-covered square was empty.

It was Nick again who came to the rescue. "We had better go to the hotel across the way; people keep off the street at night." At the hotel a sleepy porter showed us to rooms, but there was no heat, no hot water for a bath, only one electric light, and nothing to eat until nine. We sat in our big cold rooms. From our windows we looked out on the empty square. There was an ominous silence. The place was pregnant with hidden life. Shiveringly we waited for the dawn. What it would bring, we knew not.

Chapter III
TURBULENT RUSSIA—DAILY LIFE

Dawn rose over the city. I waited for what it would unfold. Petrograd was in the throes of revolution. The working class had risen. The extreme left of the Socialists, the Bolsheviki, had gained control.

I sat on the broad window ledge of my hotel window and gazed out at the silent snow-covered square. At seven, two hours before daybreak, the city began to stir. Great lines of people formed. Weary, ragged soldiers stood a block long before tobacco shops. Women with shawls about their heads and baskets on their arms appeared before provision stores. The trams began to move. They overflowed with people. Soldiers climbed to the car roofs and sat there. Women as well as men struggled for a foothold on a car step and held on to one another.

At nine, when the sun came over the horizon, the city throbbed with life. Little processions of men and women passed arm in arm under red flags, singing. There was the beat of drums and some Kronstadt sailors swung into sight.[1] Everywhere there was movement and action, but no violence. People stopped to argue. Voices rose high and arms waved wildly. It was a people intensely alive and intensely intelligent. Every one had an opinion. It was my first glimpse of Russia. My heart leaped up.

These people had not been contaminated by proximity to German militarism. They were not cogs in a machine. In spite of suppression they were not servile. They were alive and free. Continually that first impression was verified. Every Russian I met could talk. Those who couldn't read or write could talk.[2]

---

[1] Kronstadt, located on an island thirty kilometers west of St. Petersburg proper, was the traditional base of the Baltic Fleet. It was also the site of repeated violence during the revolution and Civil War; during the Petrograd riots of the February Revolution, Kronstadt sailors joined the revolution and executed officers. During the Civil War, they participated on the Red side—until 1921, when they rebelled against the Bolsheviks, an event that convinced some of those who initially supported the Bolshevik Revolution (most famously the anarchists Emma Goldman and Alexander Berkman) to condemn it.

[2] Doty's discussion in this chapter is significantly different from the version of events that she published in the British weekly *The Nation*: in the latter, Doty recalls having spent ten days holed up in her hotel room, recovering from her cold. Thus, we learn that all of the information about revolutionary events was communicated to her by Nick or by other Americans who came to visit her in he room. The *Nation* piece also gives a stronger sense of the violence, chaos,

But life in Petrograd for a stranger was difficult. The hotels were bourgeois and capitalistic. They received scant help from the working class government. There was no heat in my room and only one electric light. The food grew poorer day by day. Attempts to remedy defects by fees were useless. The waiter pushed back my tip proudly and said, "We don't take tips now." A sign in one restaurant read: "Don't think you can insult a man because he is a waiter by giving him a tip." I saw the world has been turned upside down. The cooks and waiters had become the aristocrats; the lawyers, bankers, and professors, the riff-raff.

I shivered in my room and added coat after coat. The cold—which I had contracted coming across Siberia—grew worse. But there was nothing to do but grin and bear it. The doctors had fled or were in hiding. It was only after a twenty-four-hours' struggle I secured a doctor, and when he arrived he could be of little assistance. The drug stores were closed. It was impossible to have a prescription put up. The chemists had gone on strike. They refused to work under the Bolsheviki.

But in a week the government brought the recalcitrants to terms. It threatened to take over the stores unless the chemists did business as usual.

Life was a continual battle, as it always has been between the people who have and the people who haven't. Only now it was the capitalists and the employers who were struggling for a foothold and the working class who were ruthlessly censoring, suppressing the press and imprisoning. The first revolution was political, the second economic. The working people had risen. Three things they wanted—peace, bread, and land. The Provisional Government under Kerensky had given none of these things. Instead, war was continued and an offensive was planned. This was too much for the weary Russians. No one wanted to fight. Besides, the Provisional Government failed to live up to its promises. It couldn't. It was torn between two factions, left and right. It never came to an agreement.

The land remained undivided: the people went hungry. Then the workers grew restless. They saw their dreams of peace, bread, and land no nearer. Silently they massed, and one night while the city slept one government was wiped out and another took its place. It was done quietly. In the Winter Palace the ministers of the Provisional Government sat and debated. Outside the Bolsheviki (workmen and soldiers) gathered. They barricaded the streets leading to the railroad stations with barrels, wagons and automobiles, and soldiers with bayonets guarded the barricades. Meantime the leaders of the Bolshevik movement assembled at Smolny Institute (formerly

---

and looting going on in the city. Doty may have made an effort to tone down her discussion of random violence in this later version of the piece because she feared that reports exaggerating the violence would contribute to the chaos and doom the new government, which she was critical of but also not yet ready to write off. It is also striking that the version of events in *Behind the Battle Line* makes Doty seem more independent than she was; the *Nation* piece makes it clear that, especially early on in St. Petersburg, she relied heavily on assistance from friends and acquaintances.

an aristocratic girls' school) and made it the new seat of government. Cannons and guns were mounted about the Institute. Then over the wires orders went to the soldiers in the streets. Shells began to burst over the Winter Palace. The patter of machine guns and the thud, thud of bursting shells broke the night's stillness. The State Bank, the telephone and telegraph stations were quickly seized and the small Kadet Corps guarding them overpowered. A thousand members of the Kadet Corps and the Woman Battalion guarded the Winter Palace.[3] In a few hours they were forced to surrender and the ministers were seized and sent to imprisonment in the Fortress of Peter and Paul.

At three A. M. Petrograd was in the hands of the Bolsheviki and Leon Trotsky was presiding over the All Russian Soviet (congress of workers and soldiers) at Smolny Institute, and addressing its members as follows: "We are standing before an experiment unheard of in history, of creating a government with no other aim than the wants of the workingmen, peasants and soldiers."

At seven-thirty A. M., when the first sign of the day's activities began, Petrograd presented its usual appearance. Streets were being cleaned, trams began to move, and long lines of people appeared before the provision shops. It was as though the Revolution had never been. But in reality society had turned a complete somersault. On the underside were the monarchists, capitalists, landowners, employers, skilled artisans, bourgeoisie and intellectuals; on the top, the soldiers, peasants and workers. There was a clean cleavage between the two groups. Probably in no other country could there have been such a revolution. For no other country has so consistently abused the working class. The Russian worker had nothing to lose. The peasant has lived from hand to mouth. He has gone without shoes and without meat. He has been flogged and imprisoned. Seventy-five per cent of the country had nothing to lose and everything to gain, and they turned Bolshevik. They took to the Revolution greedily. Unfortunately in many cases it meant to the individual a chance to get even, a chance to grab, instead of an opportunity to create heaven on earth. As a result the change in power brought no spiritual regeneration. Instead each group assumed the character and faults of its predecessor. The capitalists resorted to strikes and sabotage, and in every way impeded and hindered the new government. The proletariat on the other hand became dictators, and retaliated with punishment and imprisonment. One dictatorship gave place to another and the class hatred was as great as before.

Into this maelstrom I had come. What the next moment held no one knew, but each moment a counter revolution was expected.

---

[3] Doty here refers to the Women's Battalion of Death, discussed in the introduction. The unit of approximately 139 women guarding the Winter Palace is the most famous example of a female regiment's efforts. These women were among the military's last holdouts in defending the imperial regime. On the morning after the coup, Bolsheviks arrested members of the Women's Battalion, but they were released thanks to prodding by the British embassy on their behalf.

Truly Petrograd was no place to be ill in. The nights were the worst. As I lay in my bed and waited for the dawn my nerves played me tricks. I couldn't sleep. There was no one to speak to, no one who spoke anything but Russian. If I rang my bell, no one answered. I lay and shivered and waited for street fighting to begin. When the machine guns opened fire, what should I do? I seemed to hear the bullets whizzing through the window. If the soldiers entered to search or loot, would they spare me? How was I to explain I was an American and a worker and not a capitalist?

But as the days passed and no counter revolution came, my fears vanished. Often I gazed from my window and always I saw a great surging mass of people, and the more I looked the better I liked the people. They were so alive and eager. By this time I had made friends with the maid. I learned to say "Tavarish" (comrade). I would point to myself and say Tavarish. It always brought a smile and the most ready service.

This gave me a clue to the way to behave. When you are under a working class government live like the workers.

I decided to give up the hotel and find a home in a working class family. The decision was a wise one. The hotel was very expensive. In the apartment I went to I had more heat, more food and better care for one-tenth the money. From that minute forth I never had any personal difficulty. The soldiers and workers took me into their midst without question. Often I was on the street until midnight, but no one molested me; I had only to smile and say "Amerikanski Bolshevik Tavarish" (American Bolshevik Comrade) to have a hundred hands stretched out in aid. I got caught in great crowds and was unafraid. The average Russian has a dual personality—he is both a brute and an angel. But if you expect him to be an angel he'll be one. Many foreigners experienced great hardship in Petrograd and went home with wild stories, but much of the difficulty was of their own making.[4] You don't wave a red rag at a bull if you want the bull to behave. And it isn't wise to wear a high silk hat, a fur coat and a diamond ring and swagger up to an unfed, illy clothed Bolshevik and tell him he's a rascal.

Every day on nearly every street corner a fur-coated gentleman and a soldier would be in hot argument. In the end it always got down to the same practical basis:

Soldier: "You are a capitalist."

Gentleman: "You are a rascal."

Soldier: "Capitalists are enemies of the people. All must be poor, all must be alike. Where did you get that fur coat?"

Gentleman: "None of your business."

---

[4] There were wildly differing reports circulating in the United States about conditions in Russia during and following the Bolshevik coup, and conflicting reports were sometimes voiced in the same conversation, as in the 1919 Overman Committee hearings before a subcommittee of the Senate committee on the Judiciary investigating Bolshevik propaganda in the United States.

Soldier: "Yes, it is. It is our turn to have the fur coats and we are going to have them."

Sometimes on dark nights the fur coat changed hands, but usually the soldier and gentleman merely parted in hot anger.

One night the correspondent Jack Reid [sic] was held up and robbed. But he knew a few Russian words and explained he was an American and a Socialist. Whereupon his possessions were promptly returned, his hand cordially shaken and he was sent off rejoicing.[5] Another night a woman was held up and robbed. She was a Russian and explained pathetically that her home was far distant and she needed car fare. Her appeal had effect. A rouble was returned to her with the following instructions: "If any soldiers start to rob you again just tell them that Comrade So-and-so has already robbed you, but has left you a rouble to get home with."

Certainly Petrograd was not a place to live in if you wanted a peaceful and luxurious life. It was a continual fight to get the bare necessities. The days there was heat there was no light. If the electric light worked and you had heat you ran short of food. There was the intense cold to combat; the temperature stood on an average at twenty degrees below zero. One was thankful to get one thing a day accomplished. The cars were so crowded that frequently one had to walk miles in the snow-covered streets. Daily I grew tougher. The buttons got pulled off my clothes and remained off. I ceased to feel baths were a daily necessity. I grew thankful for coarse but nourishing food. There was plenty of tea, a fair amount of black bread, quantities of vegetables, cabbages, beets, carrots, turnips, potatoes and coarse meat. There was never any sweets or pastry, but sometimes we had butter and usually four lumps of sugar a day. It was a case of survive if you can and if you do you'll grow strong. And there was one great joy about life in Russia. It was thrillingly interesting. You could not be bored. Every day the Bolsheviki issued some new decree. One day all titles were abolished, the next judges and lawyers were eliminated. They and their knowledge were held to be useless. I confess to a wicked delight on that occasion. I am a lawyer and know how little justice there often is in the law.[6]

---

[5] Doty does not mention it in this version, but in *The Nation* she explains that she was with John Reed (whose account of the Bolshevik Revolution, *Ten Days That Shook the World*, is one of the most famous ever written) and his wife Louise Bryant (who was also a journalist) during these early days. See John Reed, *Ten Days That Shook the World* (Bloomington, IN: Slavica, 2018).

[6] In her piece in *The Nation* (a socialist paper), Doty also mentions that divorces were made available to anyone who wanted one. That Doty does not mention this fact about divorce in her book suggests a concern that sharing information about the ease of divorce might incline American readers to associate the Bolshevik regime with immorality, which was already happening by the time she was writing her book.

But such deeds frightened the Monarchists and Liberals. They would come out from hiding and make a show of resistance and then scurry back.[7] For day by day the Bolsheviki grew in power. All the soldiers were Bolsheviki and they had the bayonets. I used to feel I was living in a dream or had become Alice in Wonderland. In the few automobiles rode collarless workingmen, while on the street trudged an angry and puzzled banker. Petrograd became a city of working people. Duchesses and ladies-in-waiting wore aprons and wrapped shawls about their heads to hide their identity.

In the midst of this passionate life the poor Bolshevik Government had no easy task. It had let loose the brute force of Russia.[8] It was the greedy brute who caused the trouble. He looted gayly and thoroughly while the government struggled desperately to bring about order, and these looting episodes were seized on and magnified by the opposition to discredit the Bolsheviki and spread terror.[9]

My first experience of looting I shall never forget. I had been out to dinner. I had heard shooting at a distance, but hadn't realized what it meant. It was when I started to go home about eleven that the sound of bullets began to beat in on me. My way lay in the direction of the shooting. The fatal thud, thud grew almost unbearable. Then there came shouts and cries of distress. I confess I was a coward. I was with an American correspondent and his wife and I shamelessly begged them to see me home.[10] I might be willing to die for a cause, but I didn't want to be killed by a stray bullet. With great difficulty we secured a sleigh. The driver was very loath to go in the direction

---

[7] In her article in *The Nation*, Doty's wording suggests greater contempt for Monarchists and Liberals, and also gives more emphasis to popular support for the Bolsheviks.

[8] Doty's *Nation* version adds additional sentences here emphasizing pent up anger among the Russian masses. Again, that she later pared back this material suggests that she had concerns about over-emphasizing the revolution's violent nature when addressing American readers.

[9] The *Nation* version phrases this differently: "And these looting episodes were pounced upon and magnified by the Monarchists in order to spread terror of the Bolsheviks and bring about a counter-revolution."

[10] As mentioned in an earlier note, in the *Nation* version she mentions that she was with John Reed and Louise Bryant; it is not just notable that she took out their names in the book version, but also that she left Bryant unnamed in both versions—describing her only as the "wife" of this "American correspondent" or "American writer"—when Bryant, whom Doty knew reasonably well, was herself a correspondent. There may have been a rivalry between the two women; in March 1917, Bryant published an article that was somewhat mocking in its tone toward the Women's Peace Party, in which Doty was active. Bryant's articles on Russia also began appearing in the American press before Doty's, with Bryant's series of articles syndicated in American newspapers beginning April 7, 1918. Although Doty's pieces began appearing in *The Nation* around the same time, it was not until June that her writings on the revolution appeared in the American press. It also may be that Doty took out mention of Reed's name in the book because, by the time she was putting her book together, both Reed and Bryant had become controversial figures due to their unabashed support for the Bolsheviks.

we ordered. He said the shooting came from the Winter Palace, that soldiers were looting the Czar's wine cellar. It was a wonderful night, bright with stars. The sled glided swiftly over the hard snow. It seemed impossible men could be killing one another. Then a sleigh dashed past us. It evidently carried a wounded man, for he kept crying out, "Help, comrade, help." I shivered and held on to my companions. Then we came to the great river Neva, so white and silent in its winter coat of ice. On either side of its banks stood picturesque buildings and a little way below the bridge we were crossing was the Winter Palace. The shots had grown very loud now. We could see soldiers running. Their guns had been taken from them. They were shouting and screaming. Our sleigh passed close by them, but they made no move toward us. My companions said something about going to see the excitement, but I wanted to get home and bury my head under the bed clothes.

In the morning I had more courage. Besides, the shooting had ceased. I walked from my house toward the Winter Palace. When I came within two squares I saw bright red drops on the snow. At first I thought it was wine, but it was too red and thick for that, and there were splotches of red on some of the buildings where a wounded man had been leaning. All over the road and on the frozen Neva were smashed bottles. I picked up a bottle. Its label bore the Czar's coat of arms. It was a choice brand of Madeira. When I reached the Winter Palace I found it was guarded by a ragged crowd of factory boys in civilians' clothes, carrying bayonets. They were some of the Red Guard. They at least were sober. Wine is hard to get in these days, and vodka unattainable. Consequently the thirsty Russians grow desperate. That is what had happened the night before. Thirty soldiers got into the wine cellar and held an orgy; other soldiers came to drive them out and remained to drink. Quarreling began. Kronstadt sailors and Red Guards arrived, the drunk and half-drunk refused to leave. Firing began. Tempers rose higher and higher and a small battle ensued. In the end the hose of a fire engine was turned on, all the bottles in the wine cellar were smashed, and the place flooded. Three soldiers were drowned in the wine, and between twenty and thirty killed and many wounded. But with daylight order came and shame and repentance. The Russian is always very repentant. He may murder a man, but afterwards he will feed and clothe the child of the man he has murdered.

It was difficult in these swift moving days to see clearly. It will take time to see the Russian Revolution in just proportion. But one thing grew apparent. That is that in a bloody revolution where force is the basis, as in bloody war, everything fine gets pushed to the wall. Art, science, and social welfare vanish. The working class fought for power and became dictators. They ruled not by the vote, but by force. They pulled existence down to the conditions of the poorest workingman. They failed to live up to their ideals of beauty, brotherhood, fair play and freedom. Yet, while we condemn, there is this to remember: The Bolsheviki were in the throes of their struggle. Conditions will change and modify. The Russians are a brave, free-thinking people. They are democrats. They have no taint of German militarism. It is with them America belongs.[11]

---

[11] The *Nation* piece ends on a somewhat different note. Although both pieces note the high costs of a violent revolution, in *The Nation* (a left-leaning newspaper), Doty acknowledges her original excitement about and support for the revolution. In *Behind the Battle Line*, Doty is more critical of the Russian working class. The *Nation* piece also acknowledges Doty's original plan to study Russian women, as noted above. After commenting on the women, Doty adds that she was "keen on revolution" when she went to Russia, but was shocked by the violence when she saw it, and wished for a better solution; still, she notes, "People change and grow, and you can't beat, abuse, underfeed, and suppress without the lid flying off as it did in Russia." Nations must, she concludes, "make laws that will place life higher than property and insist on freedom in all things as the divine right of man."

Chapter IV

THE HUSKS OF RUSSIAN ROYALTY

"Stop off and have afternoon tea with the Czarina," said the magazine editor as he bade me good-by.

"Why, yes," I said a little vaguely, "I'd like to, but isn't Siberia rather large?" To American journalists all things are possible. But after twelve days on the Pacific Ocean and twenty days and nights of train travel through Japan, Corea, China, Siberia and Russia, the Czarina looked like a needle in a haystack.[1]

Besides, the Bolshevik revolution had descended upon me. The one hope was to be as plebeian as possible. I destroyed all my letters to people of prominence. A journalist these days must be both a Dr. Jekyll and a Mr. Hyde, a lightning change artist, who will fit with either a king or a Bolshevik.

To associate with the Czarina in Russia was like talking to a member of the I.W.W. on Rockefeller's front lawn.[2] It would have meant off with my head.

I decided to let the magazine editor have tea with the Czarina. But if I could not hobnob with royalty I could at least see their dwelling places. The Winter Palace in Petrograd was a disappointment. Outwardly it was impressive, but inside, constant use had robbed it of its glory. There were marks of muddy feet, silk hangings had been torn down to wrap about freezing soldiers, royal bedrooms had been turned into offices; one had the impression that the Czar was long since dead and buried.[3]

---

[1] After Tsar Nicholas II was deposed, he and his family spent five months under house arrest at an imperial residence near Petrograd, but fears of a monarchist uprising led Kerensky to send them to Tobolsk in western Siberia. Here they moved into the governor's mansion where they lived in reasonable comfort. When the Bolsheviks took power, they initially ignored the Romanovs, but Lenin eventually decided that it was too risky to keep the family around as anti-Bolshevik sentiment began to flare. The entire family was murdered in July 1918. However, the Bolsheviks at that time only announced that Nicholas had been executed; for several years, they successfully hid the fact that the entire family had been murdered.

[2] The Industrial Workers of the World, or IWWs, were a radical labor organization advocating "one big union." They were the target of significant repression beginning around this time.

[3] The Winter Palace was the official residence of Russian monarchs from 1732 to 1917. After the tsar was deposed, the Winter Palace became the seat of the Provisional Government; its storming by Red Army soldiers and sailors became the defining moment in the Russian Revolution, as depicted in Sergei Eisenstein's 1927 film, *October*. Bessie Beatty and Louise Bryant

I decided to go to Moscow. The Kremlin, it was said, had remained untouched. It contains perhaps the most gorgeous palace in the world. But to travel in Russia is not easy. Soldiers have precedence. They crowd on and off trains and occupy all the seats. They have even been known, when they passed their own home, to pull the danger signal and hop off. After all, why shouldn't trains be used like automobiles? But it makes travel slow. The trip from Petrograd to Moscow took twenty hours.[4] On each train is an "international wagon-lit." But berths in these cars are sold weeks ahead for a fortune. At the last moment I secured a place for myself and my interpreter in the international car. It was a woman's four-berth compartment. There was a Russian woman in a Red Cross costume in with us, and an unoccupied upper berth. Women travelers are rare, but an unoccupied berth rarer.

Presently a Russian merchant was knocking on our door. He insisted on rooming with us. We blocked the door and refused admittance. He fought for a while, but at length gave in. We were three to one.

By this time the Russian woman had grown very friendly. She said she wore her costume as a disguise, for she belonged to the aristocracy.

We stretched out on the sofas. Berths were not made up. To go regularly to bed was capitalistic. When the Russian woman found I was an American she talked freely. She was very bitter over her fate. "I don't dare go anywhere," she said. "I belong to the landowning class, or did, for everything has been taken from us. Our estate in the country, the land, the house, the furniture, was seized by the peasants. I had some jewels in the bank in Petrograd. I went to get them. I thought I could pawn them, but the Bolsheviki had taken the banks. They wouldn't give me my jewels. I have a thousand roubles in cash. It's all I have in the world. My husband is a lieutenant in the army. But the officers have been reduced to the ranks. He has to eat and sleep with the men. He gets a soldier's pay, eight roubles a month. Each day I fear he will be killed."

"But what are you going to do?" I asked. "How can you live?"

"I don't know," she said. "When my money is gone, go out as a domestic. It is the only work I know."

Again I had a bewildered sense of a turned upside down world. I felt I ought to hurry back to New York and get the Charity Organization Society to do work among the nobility.

There was the pathetic case of the first lady-in-waiting to the Czarina. She was still living in her palace. It had not been taken from her, but no one dared associate with her. Skirts were held high when she passed. One day when I was visiting Maxim Gorky his telephone bell rang; it was the first lady-in-waiting. She had telephoned to

---

were able to enter the Winter Palace immediately after its occupants surrendered, and found the place basically in tatters, though Beatty claims it wasn't as bad as they'd expected to find it.

[4] Today, high-speed trains make the trip possible in 3½ hours; by automobile, the trip is about 9 hours.

Marie Andrievna, Gorky's wife.[5] This is what she said: "I am so lonely, no one will speak to me; can't I come and see you?" The Gorkys really believe in brotherhood. They will help any one in trouble, whether it is a countess or a workingman, so Marie Andrievna telephoned back: "Yes, of course, come at once and stay as long as you like." It was this kind of deed that subjected the Gorkys to arrest.[6]

But to return to the train. I reached Moscow safely, though the trip back was not so easy. We had first class tickets, but that meant nothing. All classes are the same these days.

My first visit in Moscow was to the Kremlin. It was formerly as much a holy of holies as the palace of the Chinese Emperor in Peking. It has courtyards within courtyards and buildings within buildings. The great main gateway was shattered to bits by machine gun fire during the revolution, and the walls are battered with bullets. But inside little damage is visible. The Bolshevik commandant of the palace was a scrubby workingman, in a dilapidated suit. He hesitated some time before giving me a pass. The rooms, he said, had been sealed. But finally he scribbled something on a scrap of paper.

The untidy, unshaven little man had ordered Prince Odoviesky to show me about. We made our way to the prince's apartments. It must be trying to a prince to have to obey orders. Still it was probably pleasanter showing off the palace than being interned in the Fortress of Peter and Paul.[7] The prince was a courtly gentleman. I started to shake hands, but he blushed and ignored the outstretched hand. I don't know whether it was because he was a prince, or because since the days of the Bol-

---

[5] It is interesting that Doty refers to Andreyeva as Gorky's wife, given that she was well aware that Andreyeva and Gorky were not legally married.

[6] Although Maxim Gorky was often hailed in the Soviet Union as an icon of the revolution, his relationship to the Bolsheviks was, in fact, quite ambivalent. As noted in the introduction, in the early 1900s Gorky toured the United States on behalf of the Bolsheviks' predecessors, the Social Democrats (during which time Doty got to know him), and as a popular writer with significant earnings, Gorky lent them material support. However, Gorky was critical of the Bolsheviks' dogmatism, and he blamed them for inciting violence among the Russian masses, views that resonated with Doty's. Her remark about Gorky being in danger of arrest suggests he was already on shaky ground as far as his position with the Bolsheviks by 1918. Still, during the Civil War, Gorky was able to use his influence with the Bolsheviks to save a number of intellectuals from persecution in the Red Terror, and he also took pity on several members of the old aristocracy (not just their servants, as in Doty's example). By 1921, a number of factors, including the Bolshevik response to the Kronstadt uprising, convinced Gorky to leave the country, and he did not return until 1928.

[7] The Fortress of Peter and Paul was established in 1703 and meant to serve as a citadel to protect the city against attack, but it was used primarily as a base for the city garrison and a prison for high ranking political prisoners. It continued to be used in this capacity under both the Provisional Government and during the early period of Bolshevik control.

sheviki he has been an outcast and no one has condescended to shake hands. I almost think it was the latter, for when we left he held out his hand quite cordially.

The prince instructed one of the old court servants to take us through the buildings.

First we saw the resplendent little chapel where the Czarina used to pray. Then we went through the gorgeous guest rooms used for foreign ambassadors. They were as they had been, marble baths and all. Nothing had been changed. But now the rooms were icy cold and empty, and there was a bullet hole through one of the windows. That bullet hole was a mystery. The bullet had never been discovered.

Next we visited the throne room and ball room. The splendor was staggering. Untold wealth must have been wrung from the peasants to pay for it. On the wall behind the throne was a gigantic gold sun whose golden rays extended in every direction. The throne seemed to spring from the sun's center. It made a fitting background for a Czar. Beyond the throne room stretched the long supper hall.

Here many gay dinners had been given. In the little alcoves all down the room were piles of elaborate furniture. Beds, bureaus, tables were mixed together indiscriminately. These were treasures taken from other palaces and estates for safekeeping. The Kremlin had become a storehouse. The old retainer who showed us about was very proud of the place. He was eager to explain each item. He showed us the old wing, a portion of the building that has come down through the ages. It was Byzantine in style, with gaudy colors. The equipment was simple. The Czar of those days was satisfied with a bedroom, sitting-room, dining-room and throne-room. None of the rooms was larger than a modern drawing-room.

The personal suite of the recent Czar was not visible. Most of his furniture had been sent to him at Tobolsk. But we saw the Czarevitch's apartments. This was a palace in itself. There was something uncanny about the place. The rooms were still warm. An eiderdown puff lay ready on the royal bed, the clock on the mantel still ticked. Everything seemed ready for the young master's return. One felt each moment there would be a blare of trumpets and the royal party would enter. We asked the old servant if he liked the royal family. "Yes," he said, "they were good to me. They were kind employers. I have nothing against them."

Before we left we passed the main entrance to the palace. A great marble staircase led from the front door to the main upper hall. Up these stairs had poured thousands of courtiers, ladies in evening dress on their way to a royal ball, or nobility and ambassadors hurrying to the throne-room to listen to a royal speech.

Directly at the head of the stairs facing all who entered was a huge oil painting. It was a picture of the Czar's grandfather, addressing the peasants. In proud and arrogant grandeur he stood there, while before him, bowing low, cringed the peasants, hats in hand, and underneath the picture were written the words of this former Czar, "I am glad to see you. I thank you for your courtesy. When you return home thank my people for me, but tell them not to believe any stupid rumors about the distribution of land and the giving of it to the peasants. These rumors are lies, spread by our enemies. Property is sacred."

What a change had come! By a mighty swing of life's pendulum the land had been wrested from the nobility. Never again would it be called sacred. The unhappy recent Czar has had to pay for the sins of his fathers. It is time we invented some new mottoes. We should change "Think before you speak" to "Think about your great-grandchildren before you speak."

Poor Nicholas II must have had some bitter moments before he was led out to execution. Perhaps it flashed through his mind, "If only father and grandfather had been different this would never have happened."[8]

---

[8] Although earlier in this chapter Doty discusses the possibility of interviewing the tsarina, it is clear that this bit of the chapter, though referring to events taking place while Doty was in Russia, was written after the imperial family was executed. She may not have known that the tsar's family was executed along with him, as the Bolsheviks kept this secret for several years.

Chapter V
REVOLUTIONARY JUSTICE

I woke to find that judges and lawyers had been abolished. Over-night, legal learning and ancient precedents had been cast into the scrapheap. It was refreshing to start with a clean slate. Russia was no longer bound by traditions. Still, humanity had not reformed overnight. There were people who would grab and lie and betray their fellows. What was to be done with them?[1]

In the early days of the Revolution there had been a great jail-delivery. Many thieves and murderers, as well as political offenders, were released. Every now and then a man was caught preying upon society. The Bolshevik mob had scant mercy for such a one. They had given him freedom, and this was his gratitude. The culprit should pay the price.

A member of the American Military Control in Petrograd told me of the following incident as one he had witnessed. A woman dashed into the street after a boy of fifteen. "He's stolen my pocket-book; he's stolen my pocket-book!" she cried. A miserable shrieking urchin sped madly down the road in front of her. He was caught by passers-by, and a crowd gathered. Blow upon blow fell upon the defenseless head. Childish shrieks of terror filled the air. The woman, appalled at what she had done, rushed back to the house. Again she made a desperate search, and suddenly in a dark corner she unearthed the missing pocket-book. Again she dashed into the street, waving her property and calling loudly her mistake. But it was too late: the childish cries were still; a beaten and lifeless body had just been hurled into the canal. Sick shame seized the mob. Rage surged in their hearts. Under the Tsar they had been mercilessly beaten and abused. Brute force had been their instructor. They turned on the woman and applied the only method they knew. They beat her to death and dropped her into the canal.

Dire deeds were said to go on behind the grim walls of the fortress of Peter and Paul. Here ministers and generals languished in cells formerly occupied by ardent revolutionists. Each day a wholesale killing was predicted. But the Government was trying to suppress mob violence. A Revolutionary Tribunal had been created. People's courts with workingmen for judges were administering a crude justice.

---

[1] New courts were run according to the principle of "class justice," whereby judges elected by workers passed judgment on members of the capitalist or "exploiting" class.

With a good deal of difficulty I secured permission to visit the fortress. My permit read for seven in the evening. I took with me a young woman as interpreter. The grim fortress is surrounded by a massive stone wall and stands on the bank of the Neva, opposite the Winter Palace. At the entrance soldiers were gathered about a campfire. Camp-fires burn all over Petrograd. Wherever soldiers stand on guard they build a fire for warmth. At night the burning logs make the city bright. It is like an armed camp.

In the firelight the great iron-studded wooden gate of Peter and Paul looked like the entrance to a medieval castle. About the door, rough-looking soldiers, in long coats that came to their ankles, and shaggy fur hats, leaned on their bayonets. When I entered, and the massive gate clanged to, I felt indeed cut off from the world.

Through the darkness of the great yard we made our way to the Commandant's office. He was not in, but untidy-looking soldiers examined my pass. I must wait, they said. They eyed me curiously and spoke to my interpreter. After a little they grew friendly and invited me to have a glass of tea. They took me into the kitchen—a long, low-ceilinged room, with a great stove at one end. There were ten or a dozen soldiers. They smoked and talked incessantly, dropping cigarette-butts wherever they stood. They were dirty, ragged, and unshaven. We sat down at a long wooden table, with a steaming samovar between us. As I grew in favor, sugar, butter, and some eatable black bread were produced. This was a treat, indeed. It was hard to realize who or where I was in that dingy kitchen in the grim fortress surrounded by rough soldiers. I felt I had fallen asleep and waked up in the midst of the French Revolution.

The soldiers were looking at me curiously. I was an American, and they wanted to know about America.

"Why has America gone to war?"

"Has President Wilson sold out to the capitalists?"

"Will there be a revolution in America?"

These were the questions poured upon me. Some of the men could not read or write, but their knowledge was extraordinary. It was plain that they had but little faith in American democracy. The belief that America had sold out was widespread. This was the work of German propaganda.

I tried to answer the questions. I tried to make them see America with my eyes. I explained that half our country is bourgeois; that there is no working class which corresponds to the Russian workman; that even the unskilled American worker has something to lose; that, in consequence, there cannot be a revolution in America, such as has occurred in Russia.

They were keenly interested. The majority saw my point. They realized that changes in America are likely to come by evolution rather than by revolution. I told them that the President led rather than lagged behind the opinion of the majority; that he was more liberal and democratic than any president we had had, except Lincoln.[2] But one man, an illiterate, was not to be convinced. There was only one remedy for inequalities. The working class must rise, whether they were a minority or a majority. The capitalists must be beheaded. He himself would like to behead them one by one. In the flickering light I seemed to see him pull out his knife and feel of it. But the other men were against such methods. They suppressed this firebrand. Their intelligence was marvelous. Many had never been to school, yet they knew about conditions in both America and Europe. Their conversation was not confined to wages and food, but dealt with world-politics.

Probably in no other civilized land are there so many illiterates. But even the Russians who cannot read or write can think and talk.

By this time the Commandant arrived, and I was led forth on my tour of inspection. The massiveness of the old fortress was impressive. The walls were several feet thick. No sound could penetrate them. The corridors were like vaults. Here one was buried alive.

My request to interview the prisoners was instantly granted. I was ushered into a cell, and the Bolshevik guard withdrew. It was a room twelve by fourteen feet in size, with a high ceiling. There was one little window far up in the wall. It was impossible to see from it, and in the daytime it gave scant light. There was a stone floor, and the walls had been whitewashed. It looked clean, but cold. There was the damp chilly atmosphere of a prison. But the one electric light shone brightly. It stood on a table by the iron bedstead. The only other furniture was a chair.

The occupant of this cell was the former Minister of Finance, a man about fifty, with gray hair and beard. He courteously offered me the chair and sat on the bed. Again I had the sensation of a topsy-turvy world. Workingmen with fixed bayonets stood at the door, while a learned Minister of Finance meekly sat on his prison-bed and talked to me. He was studying an English grammar, for he could not speak English. We talked together in French. He accepted his lot philosophically. He did not complain of conditions. He and the others, he said, were treated as political offenders. They could have food from the outside, and letters and visits from their families, and might read and write as much as they liked.

"It's the psychology of the place that is terrible," he said, as he rose and paced the floor. "We can't tell what will happen. Each moment may be the last. Personally, I am not afraid. I don't think they'll hurt me. But the others are afraid. Every hour they fear a massacre. I do not dare tell my wife this. I tell her we are all right. But it is a frightful strain." It was indeed a frightful strain. Already I was feeling it. The air was charged with intense emotion. The Bolshevik soldiers didn't trust the Minister of

---

[2] Woodrow Wilson was president at the time of Doty's writings. Wilson's racist views—for instance, he strongly endorsed the 1915 film *Birth of a Nation*, which celebrates the Ku Klux Klan—have tarred his image in recent years, but it is striking that, at the time of Doty's writings, such views would have little bearing on her view of him as a liberal.

Finance and he didn't trust them. Some day the firebrand in the kitchen might be on guard. What would happen then?

I visited other cells. I talked with a Social Democrat, a man who has fought for Russian freedom and is a well-known economist.[3] He bitterly denounced the Bolsheviki.

"Go back to America and tell them what is happening here. Tell American Socialists that the Bolsheviki are imprisoning their fellow Socialists. Nine times I was imprisoned under the old regime, and since the Revolution I have been imprisoned ten times. There is little to choose. Both Tsar and Bolsheviki are dictators. There is no democracy."

After this outburst he began to pace the floor restlessly. His eyes had a haunted look. His words were those of the Minister of Finance.

"It's the uncertainty that's so terrible. Personally, I'm not afraid. They don't dare hurt me. But the others—they are afraid. They are going to pieces. Every day they expect to be lined up and shot. It is unbearable."

In each cell it was the same. There was the queer restlessness, then the fatal sentence.

"It isn't for myself I fear, it's for the others. They are afraid."

Horror seized me. I could bear no more.

The distrust of the prisoners bred distrust in the keepers. Slowly each side was being dragged to disaster. Yet outwardly there was no sign of the inner storm. "Peter and Paul" was run on the most approved prison methods.

In addition to the single cells there were two large dormitories. In these were imprisoned army officers. I was shown these rooms. The men were smoking and playing cards. Here the tension was less. Companionship had eased the strain. In one room a Russian general rose and addressed me. He spoke in French.

"Well, madame," he said, "what do you think of Russia? What do you think of a country that imprisons its officers? I don't suppose America does that sort of thing?"

The men crowded around to hear my answer.

"No," I said, smiling. "Still, America does imprison people. It imprisons men who refuse to fight."

At this there was a delighted laugh, and the general continued: "Here, you see, it's the other way. We are imprisoned for fighting. There should be an exchange of prisoners."

Even the Bolsheviki saw the joke and joined in the laugh. Certainly it was a topsy-turvy world.

---

[3] Both the Bolsheviks and Mensheviks were part of the Social Democratic Workers' Party, but the two groups split in 1903. Doty's use of the term "Social Democrat" here is thus somewhat confusing, but the person she was speaking to was clearly not a Bolshevik. Doty had just been in Germany, where she met with the Social Democrats—socialists who opposed German militarism—and this may be why she wound up using that term.

As we turned to go, my interpreter spoke to a guard. He had been rude, had pushed the generals aside and slammed the door.

"I hope," she said, "you are good to the prisoners. Remember your own prison days and what it was like."

The man hung his head. He was like an over-grown child. "I do forget," he said, "and I grow ugly."

In that little incident lay the whole story. Power breeds tyrants. No man should have arbitrary control of his fellows. As long as there was belief in retaliation and punishment life would be ugly.

A few days later I visited the Revolutionary Tribunal. I wanted to see how law without law-books and precedents was administered. The palace of the Grand Duke Nicolas Nicolaivitch had been turned into a court house. It is a massive white stone building on the bank of the Neva, near the fortress of Peter and Paul. In the old days it was gay with music and laughter. A broad marble staircase, covered with a red velvet carpet, led to the ballroom. That room was resplendent in silk hangings, a gold frieze, and a gorgeous chandelier. It had a brightly polished inlaid wooden floor. Many gay little slippers had whirled across it. Now it was covered with the mark of muddy feet. Dust, ashes, and cigarette-butts lay everywhere. The red velvet carpet had been pulled awry. The elaborate furniture was piled up in corners. Streams of workingmen and soldiers moved in and out. An excited crowd was arguing in the corridors. The courtroom was empty. The judges had retired, angry, and refused to sit again that day. The story I got was as follows:

A man named Branson, a member of the ancient Duma, and the secretary of a league for the defense of the Constituent Assembly, had been on trial.[4]

The courtroom was filled with his friends and sympathizers. When Branson entered, he was given an ovation. The president of the tribunal called for order, but the applause and cheers continued. Then the president ordered the room cleared. Whereupon indignant cries arose. "This is not a tribunal, it is a chamber of torture. We will not leave except at the point of the bayonet."

Again the president called upon the soldiers to empty the hall. Slowly they moved forward, with fixed bayonets, but the public did not stir. The soldiers withdrew into a corner. A workingman sprang to his feet and heaped sarcasm upon the tribunal. The president threatened expulsion, but the man merely cried out, "Shoot me down; you cannot put me out otherwise." The president ordered the man ejected, but he slipped in among the spectators and took a seat. From this vantage-ground he again hurled out his taunt: "Shoot me down; you cannot take me otherwise." The public sided with the man. It was impossible to reach him without violence. The patience of the court

---

[4] L. M. Bramson was a delegate to the Constituent Assembly and was arrested as part of a group of eleven opposition leaders.

was exhausted. In hot anger the president and tribunal left. By this time the soldiers were angry, and expelled the crowd with no gentle hand.

At this point I arrived. There would be no further sitting that day, so I left; but in a few days I returned. This time I had a permit, and my interpreter.

The court was to open at two. We climbed the dirty marble staircase. The air was foul and full of smoke. Across one end of the ball-room was a long wooden table covered with a red cloth. This was the judges' bench. In front were rows of wooden benches for the spectators. On one side of the judges' bench were other seats, for the prisoners, lawyers, and witnesses. There was no order or cleanliness.

Two o'clock came and went; then three, then four, then five. If Germany attempts to systematize Russia, she will have her hands full. A Russian is never on time. At six o'clock the seven judges filed in. They were all workingmen. They had been elected by the All-Russian Soviet, the Congress of Workingmen and Soldiers. Not one of them could boast of a clean collar. The president wore a dingy business suit. One man's shirt was so dirty that it was impossible to distinguish the color. He was collarless.

No one rose to greet the court. A group of Junkers were to be tried, among them a man named Pouriskevitch, a general in the Tsar's army, one of the men who had aided in the assassination of Rasputin. Pouriskevitch is a monarchist to the backbone, and hated by the working class. He and his companions were accused of forming an organization which was to seize the government and restore the monarchy.[5]

The room was packed. The trial had brought from hiding a number of titled and wealthy people. Most of the women wore Red Cross costumes.

This was to hide their elegance. But one family, a mother and several daughters and some relatives, appeared in all their finery. They wore rings and diamond brooches and displayed expensive furs. They crowded on the bench beside me. There was not room for them all, so one of the daughters turned to me. She spoke in German (the language of the Russian court): "Will you move to the back of the room. We want this bench. One of the prisoners is a relative."

I had been in court, four hours. I had sat in my seat the whole time, to hold it. I looked up at the young woman and shook my head. She reddened with anger. Her insolence was intolerable. She seemed to have forgotten that there had been a revolution. She planted herself half on me and half on the bench. She was very beautiful, but her body was as hard and rigid as her face. I found my temper mounting. I understood the rage of the Bolsheviki at the insolence of the autocracy. I drove my elbow

---

[5] Vladimir M. Purishkevich was a right-wing politician known for his strongly anticommunist and anti-Semitic views. During the Revolution of 1905, he helped organize a militia to aid police in fighting leftist extremists. He was an outspoken nationalist, and helped orchestrate the killing of Rasputin because he believed Rasputin was undermining the monarchy. Though tolerated by the Provisional Government, Purishkevich was arrested by Red Guards for participating in a counterrevolutionary conspiracy, and was among the first people to be tried by the Revolutionary Tribunal.

with a vicious dig into the young woman. She grew furious, but she no longer had power to order me to a dungeon. She removed herself from my lap, but squeezed in close. I could make no impression and gave it up.

By this time even the aisles were full. Two cooks had come up from the kitchen. Their arms were bare and they were hot and greasy. Two chairs were brought for them by the soldiers. I sat between the duchesses and the cooks. Of the two, the cooks had the better manners.

Then there was a great craning of necks. There was a sound of tramping feet. The prisoners were being led in. In they came, between two rows of Bolshevik soldiers. They were in full regimentals. Their uniforms were covered with gold braid, and they wore a great array of medals. They even had spurs on their shining leather boots. They laughed and joked like schoolboys. The soldiers who guarded them were ragged and dirty. No two had uniforms alike. Some wore caps and others fur hats. Nothing matched. One or two had their feet bound in rags. They looked like the soldiery of a comic opera. They ranged themselves along the wall and leaned on their bayonets. The whole scene was comic.

Again I felt like Alice in Wonderland. I had swallowed a magic pill which had transformed things. Cooks and duchesses; ragged soldiers and resplendent generals; collarless workingmen and bewigged and begowned judges, had changed places. Even the gaudy ball-room, by a wave of the magic wand, had become a dirty human meeting-hall.

Laughter surged to my lips, but something in the faces of the judges checked it. The eyes of the soldiers were stern. The family next me was making signs to their Junker officer. They jested and laughed. They ridiculed the proceedings. The Junker officer lay back in his chair and stretched his feet out in front of him and grinned. Contempt for the court was in every act and look.

Suddenly I remembered the soldier in the kitchen of Peter and Paul and his words, "The capitalists must be beheaded. I should like to behead them one by one." What were these people thinking of? Didn't they realize their danger?

But now the trial had begun. Pouriskevitch had retained an eminent lawyer as his defender. A gray-bearded man in a handsome frock coat stepped forward. He had all the pomp and formality of bygone days. He was over-obsequious to the judges.

Each wave of his hand was an insult.

He bowed low and addressed the tribunal. "Most reverent and honorable sirs," he began.

The prisoners giggled. A smile went around the courtroom. But the tribunal listened with wide-open, serious eyes. They struggled to comprehend the learned legal arguments. A puzzled frown crept over their faces. They consulted one another, but the lawyer's eloquent speech flowed on.

"I am sure," he said, "that this great and honorable tribunal wishes to be just; that the learned gentlemen on the bench have no thought but justice."

The biting sarcasm failed to touch the tribunal.

They listened with child-like earnestness. It was pathetic and magnificent.

But early in the case there came an interruption. Among the prisoners was a man who was not a Junker. He had been indicted with the group of Monarchists, but he was in reality a Socialist. This man's lawyer, also a Socialist, now rose. He used no blandishments. He upbraided the tribunal. He declared that it was an outrage that his client, a prominent Socialist, should be classed and tried with the despicable Monarchist Pouriskevitch.

It was as if a bomb had exploded. The courtroom was in an uproar. Pouriskevitch, red and angry, was on his feet. "How dare a common Socialist consider it an insult to be tried with me? I am a general and a noble."

It was funny and tragic. One-half the court-room glared at the other half. The judges were bewildered. In the end they ordered the Socialist lawyer from the room. They had ignored or failed to comprehend the insults or the eminent counsel, but they understood the taunts of the Socialist. Then the tribunal consulted together. At last the president rose and announced that the court would retire, to consider whether the prisoners should be tried together or separately.

It was eight o'clock. I was faint for want of food. The tribunal might not return for hours, and then it might sit until three in the morning. I decided to leave. As I pushed my way out, I realized again the intense emotional atmosphere of the fortress. Faces were flushed and eyes angry. Hot, eager talk spurted up. There was the same battle of class against class, the same hatred, the same desire on the part of each to dominate. Only the judges had been serene. They were pitiful and great in their simplicity, their struggle to understand, their attempt to be fair.

From the Nicolai Palace I went to the apartment of Maxim Gorky. A few days before, I had been there and had met the mother of Tereschenko and the wife of Konavello. Tereschenko and Konavello were two of the ministers imprisoned in Peter and Paul.[6] This mother and wife were tortured by anxiety. In their dilemma they turned to Maxim Gorky. He was the one intellectual who had not deserted the Bolsheviki. He was doing the big thing. He criticized, condemned, but tried to help. Each day his paper, *Novaya Zhizn*,[7] laid bare the faults of the Bolshevik government. Hourly he was in danger of arrest. But his stand made his home the refuge of the oppressed. Workingmen and countesses came to him for aid. Marie Andrievna, Gorky's companion for twenty years, and in all but legal formality his wife, made a charming

---

[6] Mikhail I. Tereshchenko was a sugar magnate who served as finance minister, foreign minister, and deputy prime minister under the Provisional Government; Alexander I. Konovalov was also a merchant who served as minister of trade and industry and later as deputy prime minister of the Provisional Government. Both men ultimately emigrated from Russia.

[7] Gorky established the daily newspaper *Novaya Zhizn* (New Life) in April 1917 in collaboration with Mensheviks and uncommitted Social Democrats, but the paper published views of many different leftists, including Lenin and other Bolsheviks.

hostess. It was she who cheered the distressed wife and mother and invited them to tea. It was she who promised to visit the imprisoned men. It was she who told Gorky of Konavello's rheumatism. When Gorky heard this, he went to the telephone. Over the wire he arranged to have his doctor visit the sick man. Tears of gladness and gratitude were in the woman's eyes when they left.

When I reached Maxim Gorky's, after my day in court, I was tired and spent, but they listened to my story with interest. Then Marie Andrievna told me of her day. She had been to Peter and Paul. She had seen the imprisoned men. She had found Konavello very ill. The prisoners had been through a fiery ordeal. In a moment of rashness Konavello had written to a friend denouncing the Bolshevik government and declaring that Russia was being delivered over to Germany. This letter came into the hands of the soldiers on guard. They were enraged. They cast Konavello into a dungeon, a dark cell in the basement, where the walls reeked with moisture. When the other prisoners heard of Konavello's plight, they took counsel together. It was agreed that Konavello was too ill to survive such treatment. They decided to make a protest. Ministers, generals, and other political prisoners resolved to go on a hunger strike. They were not going to be outdone by militant suffragettes.[8]

The ministers and generals proved effective hunger-strikers. The soldiers grew worried, then enraged. They led the little community out into the yard and lined them up against the wall. "We shoot, unless you suspend your strike," was the ultimatum.

But light came to three Kronstadt sailors. They suddenly stepped forward. "What we are doing is wrong," they said. "It's against all principles of brotherhood. These men shall not be shot, except over our dead bodies."

Their courage won the day. The angel in the Russian soldier rose to the surface. The prisoners were sent back to their cells, and Konavello was released from the dungeon.

"But," said Marie Andrievna when she had finished, "another time it may not turn out that way. My heart sickens when I think of the future."

Since my return to America I have read that two of the ministers in Peter and Paul have been put to death. One, I believe, was the Minister of Finance. The night-guard entered the cells and stabbed the men. It was not an act of the Soviet government, but a deed of that wild, revengeful force which has been let loose in Russia. The pity of it! For the Russian has infinite possibilities. He can be dominated by high ideals as well as by low. But the Soviet government has no time to teach ideals. In its desperate struggle to survive, in its fight for equality, it uses autocratic methods.

---

[8] Doty's reference here is to militant suffragists in Great Britain and the United States (most of them either members of the Women's Social and Political Union in England or the National Woman's Party in the United States), who went on hunger strikes to dramatize their situation. Doty's comment reminds us that suffrage struggles were in the news at the same time as the Russian Revolution.

Only the voice of Gorky rises above the maelstrom, pleading for moderation, for patience, for fine methods as well as fine principles—pleading for spiritual regeneration as well as economic equality.[9] These are his words as they appeared one morning in his paper, *Novaya Zhizn*:

> The question is, is the Revolution bringing spiritual regeneration? Is it making people more honest, more sincere? or is man's life as cheap as before? Are the new officials as rude as the old? Are the old brutalities still in existence? Is there the same cruel treatment of prisoners? Does not bribery remain? Is it not true that only physical force has changed hands, and that there has been no new spiritual realization? What is the meaning of life? It should be the development of spiritual realization, the development of all our capacities for good.
>
> The time is not ripe for this. We must first take things over by force. That is the answer I get. But there is no poison more dangerous than power over others. This we must not forget, or the poison will poison us. We shall become worse cannibals than those against whom we have fought all our lives. It must be a revolution of the heart and brain, but not of the bayonet.

---

[9] Emphasis in original.

Chapter VI
THE SOVIETS—GOVERNMENT BY THE BOLSHEVIKI

Smolny Institute in Petrograd was a girls' school in the old days.[1] It still kept the ancient title. The ground was deep in snow when I made my first visit. The Bolsheviki had made the Institute the new seat of government. I walked up the straight driveway between snow-covered lawns. A large white wooden building stretched before me. At one end was a chapel. In the colonnaded porch of the center building soldiers stood with fixed bayonets and machine guns pointed threateningly.

Figure 5. Doty's permit to enter Smolny Institute. Madeleine Z. Doty Papers, Sophia Smith Collection, Smith College (Northampton, MA).

---

[1] The Smolny Institute was Russia's first educational establishment for girls, and the actual building Doty refers to here was constructed in 1806–08 in accordance with a decree of Catherine the Great in 1764 that established the original Smolny Institute for girls of the nobility in St. Petersburg; the school continued functioning until just before 1917, under the personal patronage of the Russian empress. The building became Bolshevik headquarters during the October Revolution.

THE SOVIETS—GOVERNMENT BY THE BOLSHEVIKI

Inside the outer entrance soldiers with bayonets halted me. I must have a pass. I fell into line among a row of people. Two young girls with short hair were giving out passes. They couldn't speak English, but I made them understand I was an American and a journalist. With a smile they wrote something on a scrap of paper. The pass was a sheet torn from a tiny note book, stamped with a rubber seal and a date scrawled across it. Any one could have faked the pass. German spies could enter Smolny Institute with ease. Even the Kaiser might have risked it.

The long white corridors were crowded. Soldiers and workingmen moved in and out endlessly. They all smoked and cigarette butts and ashes were strewn over the floor. Only a short time before little girls of the aristocracy paraded these corridors arm in arm. The large, clean dormitories were filled with little white beds, the big schoolrooms buzzed with childish talk. Now the fate of a nation was being decided within these walls.

Unshaven, collarless men littered the floor with papers and argued hotly. The schoolrooms had become meeting halls and the dormitories, subdivided by wooden partitions, offices. In the corridors were long tables piled high with radical literature. There were pamphlets on anarchism, socialism, and syndicalism. All the outcasts of society here had a hearing. The place was without formality. It had the atmosphere of trade union meetings and socialist gatherings. It seethed with intense emotion. It was unlike any seat of government ever known.

There had been no time for adjustments. On the white doors down the long corridors large numbers were scrawled in blue chalk. These numbers, with the names of the committees occupying the rooms, had been written out by hand on a slip of paper and tacked to the wall. The rooms of the commisares, the Bolshevik ministers, were equally haphazardly designated. Scribbled across a sheet of paper was the simple statement "Commissare Trotsky's Office," and this was stuck to his door with a pin.

Visions arose of the stately houses of Parliament or the prosperous Capitol at Washington, and I smiled.

But the informality was refreshing. You could speak to any one, provided you could hold them for talk. For it was a rushing world. Plots and counterplots were being unfolded. The food was running low, the city was in a state of upheaval. The Bolsheviki were having a hard fight. Their control was limited to the central government. The soldiers and workers' deputies had become the Russian Congress, or Soviet. But even this body had its difficulties. It was the first to purge itself. All members not Bolsheviki or Social Revolutionaries left.

They numbered perhaps a fourth of the whole. Their places were quickly filled by Bolsheviki. The Soviet, which represented all Russia, now consisted of only the most radical elements. Bolshevik ministers were made the executive arm of the Congress, and called the "People's Commissares."[2]

But the Bolsheviki did not control the city government. The Petrograd Municipal Duma had been elected under Kerensky. Most of the members were Kadets—Liberals.

Conflict immediately arose between the city government and the Central Power. The Municipal Duma would not take orders. It refused to recognize the Soviet. The members went on strike.[3] The National power grew angry. They declared the Duma dissolved and ordered a new election. The Commissares issued the following decree:

"All employees of government institutions who strike or sabotage in their work are declared enemies of the people. Their names will be printed in the government paper and in lists which will be posted on the walls of public buildings. All those who won't work with the people have no place among the people."

The Duma did not take its fate meekly. It refused to dissolve or consent to a new election. It maintained it had been elected by secret ballot and that no one, neither the former provisional government, nor the Bolshevik Soviet could dissolve it. A few members dissented. They were Socialists. They said public opinion had changed and a new election was just. But they were voted down. In an impassioned speech Mayor Schreider declared:

"We will remain at our post and continue to work by virtue of our right until the expiration of our term of office. We will defend to the last moment and with the last drop of blood, the rights which have been intrusted [sic] to us by the people. For us the decree of the Soviet does not exist. We recognize only that law which can be changed or modified by the Constituent Assembly." But the Central Power was not to be defied. Soldiers with bayonets entered the Duma, turned out the members and closed the hall, and a new election was ordered. The irate members were helpless. There were no soldiers to defend them. They met secretly and inserted the following announcement in their paper:

---

[2] Immediately following the Bolshevik takeover of the Winter Palace, a broad coalition of socialists walked out of the All-Russian Congress of Soviets to join in resistance to Bolshevik operations. Not long thereafter, with the Bolsheviks nominally in control of the Congress, Lenin and Trotsky forced a vote that gave Bolsheviks "the right to rule by decree," with Lenin and Trotsky breaking a tie so that the motion passed. In effect, this reverted Russia to authoritarian practices that predated the 1905 revolution.

[3] On October 26 (on the Julian calendar), the Petrograd City Duma, which included many of the moderate socialists who had walked out of the Soviet Congress, created an organization called the All-Russian Committee for the Salvation of the Motherland and the Revolution. The group began organizing sit-down strikes and planning a military uprising that was to coincide with an attack by Cossacks outside the city supporting Kerensky, but the attack was defeated.

THE SOVIETS—GOVERNMENT BY THE BOLSHEVIKI

By order of the usurpers of power, the Duma was dissolved, but it still exists. Immediately after the attack, it united in another locality and continued to work on the question of unemployment. In spite of the violence of bayonets the Duma continues to guard the city's welfare, but the population which elected us must come to our aid.

Citizens, all the liberties we have conquered are menaced.

Protest against those who trample under foot our rights.

The city is in danger from cold and starvation.

Organize meetings of protest.

Pass resolutions. At these meetings let the following be your watchwords:

Down with autocratic Commissares.

Down with stranglers of Liberty.

Down with the saboteurs of the city administration.

Long live universal suffrage, direct, equal and secret.

Long live the legal autonomy of the municipality.

Long live the liberty of citizens.

Long live the Constituent Assembly.

But Petrograd did not rally to the support of the Duma. The soldiers and workers remained faithful to the Central Government. The power of the Bolsheviki grew. In every department there were the same struggles. Many officials were Kadets (Liberals) or moderate Socialists. They refused to resign or recognize the new government. They hoped for a counter revolution. But this hope was short lived. It depended on the peasants. They as a body had not joined the Soviet. A meeting was called of the All Russian Peasants Congress in Petrograd. The first business was the election of a president. Chernov received 369 votes and Marie Spiradonova 329. Chernov is a Menshevik, a Social Democrat of the right.

Marie Spiradonova is a Bolshevik, a Social Democrat of the extreme left.

Though Chernov was elected president, it was Spiradonova's faction that grew. A week later, by a large majority, it was voted to send peasant delegates to sit with the Workers and Soldiers Deputies. The Soviet had become a Congress of Workers, Peasants and Soldiers.[4]

---

[4] Victor Chernov was a leading figure among the Right SRs, or Socialist Revolutionaries, who opposed the Bolsheviks, while Maria Spirodonova, a Left SR, was in favor of collaboration with the Bolsheviks. As Doty notes, the Bolsheviks neutralized the Peasant Assembly's power by combining it with pro-Bolshevik workers and soldiers, arresting Chernov (along with other opposition leaders), and declaring all Kadets (Liberals) enemies of the people. Spirodonova was a legendary figure among the peasants: in 1906, at the age of 22, she had assassinated a police official in Tambov Province and spent eleven years in a Siberian prison, suffering terrible abuse at the hands of police. She was freed after the February Revolution. Despite her apparent support for the Bolshevik Revolution, she was incarcerated in a mental asylum after

In the winter of 1918 the representatives of 75 per cent of the population were Bolsheviki. The other 25 percent, the monarchists, the capitalists, the bourgeoisie and the intellectuals, were without representation. They refused to remain in the Soviet and they had no voice. Chernov at the Peasants' Congress, which still continued to meet as a separate body, cried out: "Newspapers are being suppressed. Tyranny is in the land. But they cannot suppress my voice. I will speak."

He was far too popular and radical for interference. He spoke on, but his power waned. Slowly the working class government took shape. Dumas and Zemstvos the country over were abolished. Local Soviets took their place. There were village, city and district Soviets. They were made up of workers, peasants, and soldiers. The local Soviets were autonomous in local matters, but their decrees had to accord with the fundamental principles laid down by the Central Power. The District Soviets, like the Central, appointed Commissares who could aid and strengthen the small local Soviets of the district.

Meanwhile the national government steadied. It began to issue decrees. Property was the main object attacked. The right to private ownership in land was abolished. Henceforth all land belonged to the nation. It was to be confiscated and parceled out to the farmers according to the needs of each family. The distribution was to be made by the local Soviets. But the Soviets were slow. Some had not been organized. The peasants grew impatient. As in the days of Kerensky they took the law into their own hands. The rough elements seized what they wanted.

One family I visited employed a maid servant from the country. She was a crude little creature, with big rough hands and ill fitting clothes. She worshiped her employers. She kissed the members of the family when they came or went. She guarded their interests as her own. I asked her about her village. Had there been violence there?

"Yes," she said with anger in her tone, "the hooligans seized the big estate. They murdered the family, even the five year old child. They found wine in the wine cellar and got drunk. They destroyed the house, divided the furniture and seized the land. They had no right to take other people's things. The land belonged to the peasants, but not the house and furniture." She turned to her employer and said, "I work for you. Suppose I took your things. I've no right to them."

Her point of view was interesting. I asked the girl if she cared for her home. Her face became radiant. The tiny strip of land and the two-room cottage were her passion. Every penny earned went to her people. She lived for the annual two months' vacation. "My own home and my own people are the best," she said shyly. I asked her if she was a Bolshevik. "No," she said fiercely, "for they say things with their tongue, but they don't do them."

Left SRs broke with the Bolsheviks in 1918, and although she was released in 1921, she was forced to cease all political activity. She later was arrested and ultimately killed in the Stalinist purges.

In another family I ran across another country girl. She had come to the city to be a seamstress. In her village there was a big estate. The owner was popular with the peasants. A meeting was held and it was agreed not to touch him or his possessions. But as time went on temptation grew. When the owner and his family went to the city his land was seized and his house destroyed.

Another interesting decree dealt with houses and apartments. These were no longer private property. But the owner might continue to live in his house provided he occupied only a small portion. The part he retained must not exceed a rental of a thousand roubles. Worked out in practice this limited a family to one room per person.[5]

Such a decree could not be carried out. There was no machinery to enforce it. It was ignored by people in general, but when the Government needed extra rooms they went to a rich man's house and took possession. Some householders resorted to tricks. One man invited a trade union organization to occupy the parlor floor. Nightly excited voices arose from the drawing-room. The mahogany furniture was kicked and banged, but the owner kept his house unmolested.

Still another decree dealt with clothing. This was not to exceed a certain amount and a certain value. No man might have more than one fur coat. The number of blankets was limited. Every one was requested to make an inventory and surrender the extras to a soldier at the front or a shivering mortal at home. Of course lies were told. It was impossible to enforce this decree. Occasionally soldiers visited the wealthier homes. They inventoried the premises and carried off the extras. To the property owners such proceedings were heartbreaking. Capitalists and bourgeoisie turned their eyes toward the Constituent Assembly as their one hope. The Assembly was to meet on December 11th. Many members had been elected before or at the time of the Bolshevik revolution. The Constituency represented all classes. The Conservatives determined to concentrate their fight on this event.

Meanwhile the Bolshevik Government grew daily more unfriendly to the Constituent Assembly.[6] That body would be full of Kadets. Kadets were enemies of the people. At first these sentiments were uttered timidly. To supplant the Assembly with

---

[5] Jessie Lloyd O'Connor, an American heiress, socialist, and journalist, wrote in the diary she kept in a months-long stay in Moscow beginning in 1927 about a former aristocrat (working as Lloyd's translator) who, in the late 1920s, was living in what used to be the bathroom of her family's former mansion. Jessie Lloyd diary, Jessie Lloyd O'Conner Papers, box 90, folder 4, Smith College.

[6] The battle over the Constituent Assembly was one of the defining moments in the Bolsheviks' amassing of their power. Recognizing both that great popular faith had been placed in the idea of a Constituent Assembly and that they would not have a majority in it, the Bolsheviks at first delayed the assembly's meeting for as long as possible, and then ultimately dissolved it, in essence thereby giving up the pretense of representing the will of the people.

the All Russian Soviet would take time. The people had been taught to regard the Assembly as the culmination of all hopes.

The monarchists and capitalists were clever. Secretly they were hatching plots for counter revolution. Kaledine and the Cossacks were to march on Petrograd and seize the Government.[7] But these efforts except when discovered and exposed by the Commissares, were kept dark. Outwardly, the Conservatives asked for but one thing, representation. The Constituent Assembly must meet. Every one must have a voice. Shrewdly they let the radical intellectuals Chernov and Zeretelli do the talking.[8] These men were Socialists. They were Bolsheviki in principle but not in method. They believed in a revolution by the vote, but not by the sword. They were feared by the Commissares. Their power was great.

They could not be downed. The peasant was willing to behead the capitalist, but these men were loved.

Several days before the opening of the Assembly meetings were held. One Sunday morning I went to hear Zeretelli. The meeting was in a great circus. The place holds six thousand. It was jammed. Zeretelli is dying of consumption. He has spent seven years in penal servitude and given his life to the cause of Russian freedom. He is pale and thin and his eyes are sunken. No one has ever doubted his honesty and sincerity. He spoke with passion. He declared the time was not ripe for a working class government. There must be a coalition. Socialists and capitalists must unite. All must be represented. The Assembly must meet. The decrees must be made by that body. They must be the product of the vote of the whole people.

This speech brought thunderous applause. But it was not passionate applause. The meeting lacked fire. The audience was made up of doctors, lawyers, bankers, school teachers, and shop keepers. There were no factory workers and only a few soldiers present. Reason was stronger than emotion.

On December 11th there was a parade as a demonstration for the Assembly. The Soviet paper requested the Bolsheviki not to take part. I was out early and wandered about the streets. At ten the line began to form. Riots were expected. It was feared the two parties would clash. But except for a few bullets fired by an over-excited man, I saw no violence. There were ten thousand in line. A Bolshevik demonstration would

---

[7] Aleksei M. Kaledin was a leader of the Don Cossacks, which, during the first several weeks after the February Revolution, organized an anti-Bolshevik, pro-Ally rally in collaboration with General Mikhail Aleksev, commander in chief of the Russian army. Following Lavr Kornilov's failed coup from the Right in August 1917, Kornilov, joined by Kerensky's former chief of staff, Anton Denikin, teamed up with Aleksev and Kalendin to form the "Volunteer Army," the first major "White" movement in the Russian Civil War.

[8] Zeretelli (or Tseritelli) had been active in socialist politics for many years, and was imprisoned in Sibera from 1907, when Prime Minister Pyotr Stolypin dissolved the Duma, until the February Revolution. He was a prominent and well-respected figure among moderate socialists, who advocated collaborating with liberals in opposition to Bolshevism.

have brought out fifty to seventy thousand. The marchers were all well dressed. They walked and talked quietly. They sang solemnly and sincerely. They were the bourgeoisie and the intellectuals with an occasional capitalist. None of the proletariat and only a few well dressed soldiers joined. The crowd lacked passion. They did not seethe with life. They moved to the Tauride Palace, the meeting place of the Assembly. They swept up to the doors. But Bolshevik soldiers guarded the entrance and they turned back. They marched down a side street. They had no plan. I watched three men with particular interest. They were lawyers or bankers. They wore fur coats and fur caps. They and the others were singing the Marseillaise. Over their heads waved a red flag on which was written "Land to the Peasants." On the sidewalk factory workers and unshaven soldiers stood and jeered. Surely I had gone crazy. It wasn't possible that the moneyed class were marching in the middle of the street under a red flag singing the Marseillaise, demonstrating against the Government, and shouting for freedom.

At two the Assembly was to open. Only 194 of the 800 delegates had arrived in Petrograd. Of that number three dozen or so presented themselves. Those with certificates or passes were allowed to enter the palace.

The ballroom had been turned into a legislative hall. It was filled with raised seats and desks arranged in a semi-circle. The handful of members proceeded to convene. Mayor Schreider, the Mayor of the dissolved Duma, took the rostrum:

"I declare," he said, "the Constituent Assembly open."

Chernov was then elected president. He took his place and announced that three Kadets (Liberals) members of the Assembly had just been arrested.

A motion was made and carried to make public the following declaration:

"The Constituent Assembly refuses to recognize the brutal force which has arrested its members and declares those members free." Before adjourning it was agreed to meet the next day. In closing, Chernov said:

"When this body meets regularly the power will pass from the hands of the usurpers to us. It is we alone who can make peace and give land and liberty to the people. Long live the Constituent Assembly."

Next day I went back to the palace. Eight thousand soldiers had been placed in neighboring barracks. The palace itself was well guarded. Soldiers with bayonets were at every entrance. Small detachments moved about the buildings and grounds. One company was sprawled upon the floor of a big room. They had their knapsacks for head rests and were fast asleep. Several of the correspondents gathered in a corridor to talk. Immediately soldiers stepped up, and told us to move on. Meantime thirty or forty delegates straggled in. They were the professor type. They wore frock coats. There wasn't a working man among them. They were jostled by the soldiers and not allowed to form in groups. They withdrew to the library. Here they began to hold a meeting. The Commandant of the Palace appeared. He said their meeting must stop; that the council of Commissaries would announce when they could meet; that first, all Kadets must be arrested. Then a delegate jumped up. "Will you arrest a member of the Assembly?" he asked. "Certainly," said the Commandant. "If he is a Kadet, for they are enemies of the people. They are not Assembly members, only the proletariat can hold such an office."

But the little group refused to retire and the Commandant withdrew. They hadn't a quorum. It was useless to hold meetings until more members reached Petrograd. They decided to publish the following statement:

> People of Russia, do you know how the new despots treat your representatives? All the rooms in the Tauride Palace are closed. It is clear to the whole world that the promise of the Bolsheviki to speedily unite the Assembly is a lie. They make that promise to hold their power. They promise one thing and hope another. When our number increases and we are strong we will return to the palace. We will not give in to the usurpers. Be ready to fight for the Constituent Assembly.

This was signed by Chernov and 109 members. They had hardly finished when the Commandant returned with soldiers. The members were ordered out and one man was forcibly ejected. It was the last meeting in the palace. The Commissaries had taken up the fight in earnest. Trotsky and Lenine were making impassioned speeches.[9] They issued the following statement:

> A handful of people are trying to open the Assembly. They do this that they may declare their counter revolutionary actions legal. All the conquests of the Revolution are in jeopardy. The People's Commissaries bring this plot to the attention of the public.

The Commissaries had grown bolder. They began to attack the Assembly openly. They had been successful in the new Duma election. The total votes cast was only one-half of the 900,000 votes of the preceding election, but practically all the votes

---

[9] Vladimir Lenin and Leon Trotsky were the leaders of the Bolsheviks, with Lenin in charge and Trotsky as de facto second in command. Lenin (born Vladimir Ilyich Ulyanov) was from a wealthy family, but had embraced revolutionary politics at a young age. He led the Bolshevik split against the Mensheviks in 1903, and lived in exile between the 1905 and 1917 revolutions, returning to Russia in July 1917 for the failed July coup and then again in October. He died in 1924 after a series of strokes. Trotsky (born Lev D. Bronstein), from a wealthy Jewish Ukrainian family, became involved in political activity as a teenager. Starting out as a populist, Trotsky became a Marxist Social Democrat. He had supported the Mensheviks after the 1903 split, but joined the Bolsheviks just prior to the October Revolution and immediately became a leader in the Communist Party. He served as people's commissar for foreign affairs and then became commander of the Red Army. Trotsky was expelled from the Communist Party in 1927 after failed efforts of the Left Opposition against Joseph Stalin, and he was assassinated in 1940 in Mexico by a Soviet agent.

THE SOVIETS—GOVERNMENT BY THE BOLSHEVIKI

were for the Bolsheviki. The new Municipal Duma had convened and the new mayor had opened with the following remark:

"I salute the victory of the proletariat over the bourgeoisie. Greetings to the People's Commissaries. Let us proceed to socialize property. Let us carry out the decrees of the Council. Long live the Commune."

Encouraged by this spirit, the Commissaries issued two decrees. One declared all Kadets enemies of the people and demanded they be arrested immediately and brought before the Revolutionary Tribunal.

The other granted the right to a new election on the petition of one-fourth of the electors, and gave the power of recall. At a meeting at Smolny Institute of the Soviet, Trotsky and Lenine defended these decrees and their messages. Said Lenine:

"In the midst of a civil war one must not make a fetish of the Constituent Assembly. It is the bourgeoisie and Kadets who have dragged us into strife.

"Around the Kadets all counter revolutionary elements gather. Shall we then convoke the Assembly as it originally was elected? To do so is to gather together counter revolutionary forces. This must not be."

But such doctrines were not calmly accepted. Instantly a soldier was on his feet protesting.

"You cannot arrest a whole party. If you use these methods with the Kadets you will use it with others. Soon there will be no Assembly."

Then Trotsky sprang to his feet.

"It is impossible to collaborate with elements against whom we are obliged to send troops. Russia is divided into two camps, the bourgeois and the proleteriat. It is not immoral to achieve the fall of the bourgeois. You are indignant at these terroristic methods, but if they are not used, in a month, methods more menacing will be applied. It will become the terror of the French revolution. For our enemies it will not be the fortress but the guillotine."

Feeling was now at white heat. Only the Assembly was talked of. To be or not to be that was the question.

An exciting debate was expected in the Soviet or Congress. I determined to attend the meeting. Unfortunately no cars were running. The electric wires had been tampered with. It was thought to be the work of some counter revolutionary. It was four miles to Smolny Institute but I plowed through the snow. The school ballroom was the Soviet headquarters. The white walls and woodwork were growing dim. The hard wood floor had long since lost its polish. But the gay chandelier flooded the place with light. The Soviet delegates were out in full force. They were a serious and earnest body. Intelligence was writ large across their faces. They were without self consciousness. Most of the men were in dingy uniforms for both the factory workers and the peasants are all in the army. The air was thick with smoke. The place hummed with talk. The Commissaries mixed with the delegates. No extra reverence was shown them. Trotsky and Lenine pushed their way with the others to the platform. It is a genuine working class government. No official receives more than 500 roubles (at the present rate of exchange in Russia $50) a month. He may use the government automobiles, but he has to eat and sleep with the workers.

It was Trotsky who spoke first. He is a man of medium size with a large well shaped head. His hair is thick; his forehead high, his eye bright and keen. His chin is small and weak, but this is hidden by mustache and short beard. He stoops slightly. He is simple and direct in manner and without affectation. He speaks with passion and plays upon his audience's emotion. His feeling about the Assembly was tense. His words came thick and fast.

"The question of calling the Assembly is entirely different from Kerensky's time. The right of immunity of the members is raised. But there is another right that is higher, that is the right of the revolutionary people. In declaring the Kadets our enemies we have only made a beginning. We have not yet executed any one (cries of— 'We are against the death penalty'). Yes! That is true, but if the conspiracies of the Kadets and Kaledinists disorganize the country, not one of us can guarantee that in their legitimate anger the people will not turn against the bourgeoisie and the Kadets. No one of us can say that the people exasperated will not raise the guillotine in the public square in front of the Winter Palace."

At this point Trotsky's voice was drowned. The room was in commotion. Every one talked. Then a social revolutionist[10] sprang to his feet. Order was restored and he began to speak.

"However much we believe in fighting counter revolutionary forces, we cannot declare all Kadets enemies of the people and refuse to let them sit in the Assembly. To do this will end in excluding the moderate socialists. Finally there will be no Assembly. The peasants and workers look on the Assembly as the final coup, the expression of the national will. They will not understand. It will bring on bloody revolution.

"Lenine and Trotsky after making an end of Kadets will turn against their socialist friends. If in their dreams they see Marat and Robespierre, let them not forget Robespierre's end and that which came after. The Russian revolution can be pushed to the same end.

"In this chamber it should not be only words of hate that are heard, there should also be words of love. Our revolution before all else was waged in the name of justice."

Thus the battle raged. But in the end Trotsky won. The decree declaring all Kadets enemies of the people and excluding them from the Assembly was adopted by a big majority. The Assembly's fate was sealed.

I left before the vote was taken. I knew there would be a battle royal in the Peasants' Congress. They too were debating the future of the Assembly. Another

---

[10] Presumably, she means a Socialist Revolutionary, or SR, a populist group that contended for power with the Bolsheviks. Initially, the Bolsheviks agreed to share power with the Left SRs, but that collaboration had ended by 1918 after disagreement over the Brest-Litovsk peace treaty.

THE SOVIETS—GOVERNMENT BY THE BOLSHEVIKI

correspondent and myself made our way to the town hall. The cars were still not running. We were both dead tired. By a bit of luck we got a sleigh. It was biting cold, but the four miles back to the Nevsky Prospect was soon covered. We mounted the steps of the Duma building. We went in the back way. We knew the place would be jammed. No East Side Socialist gathering ever equaled that crowd for emotion. The place throbbed with the life of the whole world. The Peasants' Congress still retained Chernov and his faction. They sat on the right, the Bolsheviki on the left. It was like some great musical drama.

The rise and falls, the cadences, the stops, the streams of talk, the bursts of passion. Marie Spiradonova, a tiny wraith of a woman, controlled the left. She is adored by the peasants. Her years of torture in exile have made her a god. She can do no wrong. There were hot words and hisses, but her tiny hand quelled and quieted the great peasants.

"Let the other side speak," she kept saying, "let the other side speak."

While Chernov from his side stirred his group to new endeavor, his great head with its mass of hair waved and tossed, his fists pounded the desk. The room when I entered was in the throes of a struggle. Should Lenine be allowed to speak or shouldn't he? He pushed his way through the seething people to the platform. There were hisses, cries, bursts of applause, a maddening uproar. Chernov called loudly for Lenine's ejection. He had no right in the Peasants' Congress. Finally quiet was restored and a vote taken. By a large majority it was voted Lenine should speak. He is a small man. Not at all radical in appearance. The front of his head is quite bald. His face is clean shaven except for a small mustache. His manner is simple. He started in like a college professor reading a lecture. He didn't pound or rant. But in a few moments the crowd was still. His words burnt in. Each one came liquid clear. It was like a stream that started small and clean and grew to a deep swift running river. The man was sincere, a fanatic, but an idealist. I found myself swept along, throbbing and beating with every emotion of the great rough peasants. My reason was against what was being done. I didn't believe in winning by force. I believed in democracy. I believed every one should have a voice. The bourgeoisie were not all bad, nor the proletariat all good.

The right could be risked to the decision of all mankind. If the majority were not for it, it would not last. Not a class conscious but a world conscious decision of right was what was needed. Yet in spite of my belief I found myself shouting and clamoring with the left. It was infectious. The peasants were so simple and true. There were no ifs and buts about them. They had been beaten and abused and underfed and left to fight the Germans with naked fists. The moneyed class had betrayed them. The aristocracy had allowed Germany to flood the land, monopolize the Government and seize the business. With a mighty effort this beastly tyranny had been overthrown. Now they were told the Kadets were betraying them, they were like the moneyed class of old. Well then, down with all Kadets. The Assembly must meet, but the Kadets must go. Through all this surge of feeling, gradually the words of Lenine stood out:

"Only people without consciences can say the Bolshevik Government is a menace to the peasants. Nine-tenths of the army is composed of peasants, or to put it another way, the guns are in the hands of the peasants. It is just because the power of the Soviets rests on the mass of the people that no force in the world can go against them. The conspirators, the Kalidinists, are isolated, and they must succumb wherever they are, even if they are members of the Assembly. The people are not made for the Constituent Assembly, but the Assembly for the people. That body ought to consolidate our victory, but it doesn't. It does not reflect the opinion of the masses. Why then should you hesitate. You have not hesitated to take the land from the capitalist, why should you hesitate to take from him his vote?

"The Soviet will arrest all who do not recognize the Soviet. The Assembly will not be convoked until 400 loyal members have assembled."

For a moment there was quiet. Then came tumult.

As Lenine walked from the room the left rose. They shouted, they stamped, they cheered. It was deafening. The hisses of the opposition were drowned. But Chernov was on his feet demanding a hearing. It took some minutes to restore order. He was irritated. He spoke with heat. Somehow his words missed their mark. His gestures seemed artificial. His oratory after Lenine's simplicity was unconvincing. He seemed to be hurling rocks into a rushing stream. It didn't stem the current. Yet he had reason on his side. His words were applauded by the right, but scorned by the left. What he said was:

"The Commissaries usurp the rights of the Constituent Assembly. They do not openly agitate the dissolution of that body but proceed by underhand means. They arrest isolated deputies. If the Kadets are guilty of a plot, the Assembly itself should suspend their parliamentary immunity. Even in the days of the Czar socialist members were not arrested until the Duma had been asked to suspend immunity. But the Commissaries know no law. They push the Soviet against the Assembly. It is time the Soviet rose and demanded that these dictators, these Commissaries, return to them their power so that they in turn may place that power in the hands of the Assembly."

When he finished men sprang up all over the floor.

Hot words flew back and forth. One peasant on the left cried out: "Long live the Constituent Assembly, but if it goes against the will of the workers it is the last time I will utter that cry."

At eleven o'clock Trotsky entered. But the audience was in no temper for a speech. The left saw to defend him was useless. The right had grown ugly. They hurled taunts at Trotsky. "Down with the drinker of blood. Put him out," they yelled. Then a motion was made to demand the immediate opening of the Assembly. A violent struggle ensued but the motion passed by a vote of 360 to 321.

THE SOVIETS—GOVERNMENT BY THE BOLSHEVIKI

That night I trudged back to my house full of conflicting emotions. Russia and Russia's problems were not easy to solve. When I reached the Leteiney Prospect I hurried into my door. To be out at midnight was neither safe nor comfortable. There was only one light on each street. There wasn't fuel for more. It would have been difficult to see but for the glistening white snow. I was weary from my enforced walks. I fell promptly to sleep. Then bang, bang. I woke with a start. Another bang. I sprang from my bed and rushed to the window. The street was empty. Then I saw a couple of people running and stooping low. They dashed into the doorway of the telegraph office opposite. Then bang, bang, more shots. Instinctively I knew what it was. The soldiers were looting the wine shop on the corner. If they stuck to the wine it would be all right, but suppose in their drunkenness they besieged our apartment. My heart beat violently. We were on the fifth floor. Surely they wouldn't climb so high. But suppose they began shooting at windows. A fifth story window was a long snot. I went back to bed. The shots continued but gradually they died out. Excited voices rose from the street. What a tempestuous life it was; so full of good and ill. What would come of it? One must have patience. The changes were too great and sudden to come without violence.

By a mighty swing of life's pendulum the land had been torn from the aristocracy. No Czar could ever again declare property sacred.

But the change was too great. The pendulum had swung too far left. It could not remain there. It must swing back, that was a law of nature. Russia had swung clean out of the Twentieth Century. Whether she will come back with a rush and a counter revolution or gradually slow down and stop like the pendulum in the center is a question hard to answer. Only unselfishness and self-sacrifice can save Russia from further bloodshed and turbulence. Progress comes in two ways, by revolution and strife, by jerks forward and back, or a slow and steady march onward. The latter way is the way of an enlightened civilization. But as yet there has been no race of men great enough to achieve it. For it means that a nation must live in the present but work for the future. It means that peasant as well as capitalist must seek nothing for himself. It means that each must give of his home, his country, his life if a fair and decent world is to be built for the children of the future. The peasant in the Soviet who cried out "words of love, not words of hate, should be spoken in this Assembly," struck the right note. What Russia needs today is not more force but understanding sympathy, encouragement and love.

Chapter VII
THE GERMANS IN PETROGRAD

Should I wait until they came? I knew the things I had written about Germany made capture fatal. I had no desire to be interned in a German prison camp. Was it a delegation or a whole army of Germans that was marching on Petrograd? No one seemed certain. But it was too exciting to miss. I stayed on.[1] As a matter of fact the German delegation slipped in quietly enough. They made hardly a ripple. There were sixty Germans in all, twenty-five official delegates and thirty or more secretaries and technicians. They were lean and hungry looking and very stiff and funny. They were like posts of wood sticking out of a surging ocean. They bore no resemblance to the throbbing Russian masses. It is important to remember this in predicting future relations between Russia and Germany.

The Russians are individualists. They cannot be permanently conquered. Temporary domination will only result in the lid flying off. They are a free thinking race. Their country is full of Republican traditions. In the early days the provinces were ruled by princes elected by the people. The first Romanoff was chosen Czar by the people. It is the Germans who have foisted bureaucracy and tyranny upon Russia. The whole upper stratum of society was of German importation. Even in the days of Czarism the peasant village life was one of pure democracy. They had their town meetings or mir.[2] They discussed public affairs. They worked things out together. No one man was better than another. That is the reason that today even the Russians who can't read or write can think and talk. Contrast this with German life before the war. The German sat in his beer garden fat and content. He lived on time. He took his pleasures methodically. He obeyed those above him. To obey, to be a machine, not to think, to live on time are qualities the Slav does not possess. He eats at all hours, talks half the night, drinks tea incessantly, argues hotly and is a revolutionist at heart. When Slavs and Teutons meet something explodes.

The Russian is the dynamo, the German becomes the scattered remnants. This accounts for the great changes in Russia. The dynamo went off and the Russian bu-

---

[1] Armistice negotiations between Russia and the Central Powers began in late November 1917, and a truce was declared in early December so that peace negotiations could take place.

[2] The Russian mir was a self-governing community of peasant households that communally controlled the local lands.

reaucrat and his German brother were wiped off the map. All we need is patience and Russia will revolutionize Germany. But if such antagonism exists between the Russian masses and the German Government why was peace made?[3] There are three reasons:

First because 7,000,000 Russians had been killed or wounded and the country was bankrupt and hungry.

Second because the Russians were too busy carrying on a revolution to wage a war.

Third because Karl Marx was born in Germany and the Russians believed that if peace was made their German Socialist brothers would rise.

This accounts for Brest Litosk [sic].[4] But never for a moment was there friendship between the Russian worker and the German Government. The Russians clamored for a general, not a separate peace, without annexations or indemnities. The Kaiser listened coldly to such a proposition. He had no use for a Bolshevik Government. The German papers ridiculed Russia. On October 3rd, 1917, the Frankfurter Zeitung declared "The Democratic peace proposals of the Soviet are absolutely inacceptable to any German." But hardly had the paper uttered the words when trouble began. The German workers had heard the call of the Russians. There were strikes everywhere; 300 independent Socialists were arrested and imprisoned. In Austria there were 80 manifestations and the watchword was "Not another bullet, but immediate peace." In Budapest 150,000 people took part in a demonstration. The Kaiser was frantic. The jig was up. His days were numbered. But then he had an idea. He loathed the red flag of revolution, but if he made friends with the Bolsheviki he could fool his people. He could make them believe he wanted peace. And another brilliant idea dawned on him. If he played with the Russians he could perhaps get them to disband their army. When the soldiers had left the front and the country was disorganized he would turn and deal Russia a swift blow. He would tear down the red flag which threatened his throne and put back the Czar. So reasoned his imperial majesty. Deliberately with malice aforethought he held out a hand to the ragged fiery revolutionist. At first he egged the Russians on in their clamor for a general peace.

---

[3] Doty here is referring to the separate peace that the Bolsheviks made with Germany and the other Central Powers (Austria-Hungary, Bulgaria, and the Ottoman Empire), ending Russian participation in World War I.

[4] The treaty was known as the Treaty of Brest-Litovsk because it was signed at Brest-Litovsk, Ukraine (under German occupation at the time). Its terms were extremely harsh on Russia: Trotsky's efforts to negotiate more lenient terms resulted in Germany coming close to invading Russia again and Lenin ultimately being forced to accept terms even more unfavorable to Russia than those that were originally offered, requiring Russia to give up claims on Poland, Finland, Latvia, Ukraine, and Lithuania. The treaty was signed on March 3, 1918, which was after Doty had left Russia, but negotiations were underway while she was in Russia.

The Central Powers wanted a general peace on their own terms. Each day internal conditions in Germany grew worse. Thus it was that the Kaiser went out to meet the Bolsheviki. It was like Goliath going out to meet David. It was funny and tragic. At Brest Litosk the two delegations met. The Russian delegates were scrubby unshaven tired workingmen. They wore blouses, faded uniforms and dilapidated business suits. They were met in state by Leopold, Prince of Bavaria, General Hoffman and other dignitaries, clad in resplendent uniforms with leather boots and clinking spurs, and shining medals. This imposing array stood rigidly heel to heel and hand to cap. But the Russian worker, unabashed, stepped forward with outstretched hand and said "brother." It was like a clap of thunder. The earth shook. The Teutonic officials nearly lost their dignity. Such freedom was scandalous. It must be kept from the people. Large automobiles hurried the Russians to a hotel. There they were carefully hidden away. Soldiers were stationed about the hotel. No delegate was allowed to walk out or talk to the people. The delegates were made prisoners but royal prisoners. Everything was done to entice and corrupt them. "Will you walk into my parlor, said the spider to the fly?" They were given suites of rooms with baths. Each bathroom ostentatiously displayed a cake of soap. There was writing paper and cigarettes on the tables. But the Russian was incorruptible. He loves freedom. Physical comfort counts for little. He didn't like riding around in an automobile with a German soldier as nurse. He grew restless. He began to ask embarrassing questions. "What about Liebknecht?"[5] "Why had 300 independent Socialists been arrested?" "Why couldn't they meet the German people, they didn't want to talk to officers?" At last the ill assorted group settled down to business. The Russians began at once to talk peace. But the stiff and haughty Germans shook their heads. Only the heaven-sent Kaiser could talk of civil affairs and peace. They had come merely to discuss the technical details of an armistice. "Oh, very well," said the bored Russians, "here's our program."

1. Suspension of hostilities.
2. No renewal of war except with 3 days' warning.
3. No transference of troops from the Eastern front.
4. The space between the trenches to be neutral territory. In the neutral territory fraternization to be allowed, but no wine to be sold or drunk and no penetration of enemy trenches under pain of being made prisoner.

After much study and shaking of heads the Germans said they must have time to think the matter over.

---

[5] Karl Liebknecht was a German socialist and co-founder (with Rosa Luxemburg, Clara Zetkin, and others) of the Marxist Spartacus League and the Communist Party of Germany. Liebknecht (and the other Spartacists) were outspoken critics of German involvement in World War I.

"Very well," said the Russians, "but while you're thinking why not call all the belligerents to make peace? You say you are and always have been ready to make peace. Well then, state your terms and call on the world to join."

But the Germans, confused and embarrassed, hurried away. Before they left, Kameneff, the chief of the Russian delegation, fired a parting shot.[6] He didn't put his finger to his nose, but he did the same thing in words. This is what he said, looking straight over the heads of the Germans:

"All our proceedings are to be open. In giving out our reports we wish the mass of the German people to comprehend that we have not come to Brest Litosk to confine ourselves to an accord with German generals, but to demand of the German worker over the generals' heads that they join their voice with ours to engage the people in a fight for peace."

Meanwhile in Petrograd, Lenine and Trotsky were getting out the following manifesto for distribution in the German trenches:

Brothers and soldiers, we invite you to help us fight for peace and Socialism, because only Socialism will insure to the proletariat a solid peace and heal the wounds caused by the war.

German brothers and soldiers, the great example of your leader Liebknecht, the fight which you carry on in meetings and in the press, and above all the revolt in your navy is a guarantee that the fight for peace among the working class is ripe.

Brothers, if you will hold, peace is assured at least on the European Continent. All the other powers will join in a just and democratic peace. If you will help, we can establish Socialism in Russia, which for us to do alone is extremely difficult. Your capacity for organization, your experience, will

---

[6] Lev B. Kamenev (née Rosenfeld) had become active in revolutionary politics as a college student, and began working as a professional revolutionary after a 1902 arrest ended his formal education. He was married to Trotsky's sister, Olga Bronstein, and the family lived in and out of Russia, as Kamenev faced periodic arrests and imprisonment for his activity. Although Kamenev was prominent among the Bolshevik leadership, he had several well-known disagreements with Lenin; most significant was Kamenev's opposition to the Bolshevik seizure of power in October 1917. Kamenev was elected Congress chairman and chairman of the All-Russian Central Executive Committee at the Second All-Russian Congress of Soviets, but he and several others resigned from the Central Committee not long after the Bolshevik coup over a dispute about whether to negotiate with railroad workers, who demanded that a greater range of views be permitted in the government (Kamenev was in favor; Lenin was not). Kamenev was a leading figure in the negotiations at Brest-Litovsk. Although initially an ally of Trotsky's, the two fell out of favor, but he also became a rival of Stalin's, and was arrested and killed following the 1936 show trials.

give us the necessary means to bring about Socialism. Our soldiers will not advance one step if you will take the flag of peace in your hands.—Long live peace.—Long live International Social Revolution.

But alas! Neither this appeal nor Kameneff's words reached the German people. The Kaiser took good care of that. The German people knew only that their government was making peace with Russia and they were content.

In the Reichstag Count Hertling was saying:[7]

"We Germans follow with greatest sympathy the tragic events in Russia. Germany hopes for the return of normal conditions there and dreams of the reestablishment of the ancient neighborly friendship, especially in economic relations," and then he added, "The Russian proposals for an armistice seem possible, the looked-for peace ought soon to be an accomplished fact."

About this time a big meeting was held in the Alexander Theater in Petrograd which has an auditorium as large as the Metropolitan Opera House.

It was a meeting of the clans. The members of the All Russian Soviet, the representatives of the Peasants' Congress and delegates from the factory workers, soldiers and Red Guard were present. The place was packed. A pass was necessary to enter. I had only the statement from the American Embassy that I was an accredited correspondent. That document had an impressive red seal. I waved this pleadingly before a soldier. He let forth a flood of Russian and barred the way. But my inability to understand and my patience finally won him. He beckoned and I followed. He led the way down passages and through many doors. He was trailing his gun while I followed meekly in the rear. In a few moments I discovered we were in the rear of the theater, behind the scenes. The soldier said something in Russian and moved on. In another second we were out upon the stage. The curtain was up, the place was jammed, the speakers were already upon the platform. But this didn't trouble the soldier. Straight across the stage he went, right in front of Commissare, Trotsky, Mlle. Spiridonova, Madame Kollontai, and the other speakers, and I trailed along behind. Each moment I expected to hear jeers from the gallery. But the Russian is used to eccentricities and informalities. No one paid the slightest heed to us. When we were safely across the platform the soldier deposited me in the front row of the orchestra where the correspondents were assembled and I settled down to watch proceedings. It was like a state convention, a presidential campaign, and a Fourth of July rolled into one. The audience buzzed with talk. These people knew what they were after. They were tremendously in earnest, intent, alive. When Trotsky spoke he was interrupted by questions and comment. This is what he said in part about the peace negotiations:

---

[7] Count Georg von Hertling, former prime minister of Bavaria and a conservative Catholic, was appointed chancellor of Germany in 1917 at the age of 74.

"We cannot but regret that events do not proceed as rapidly as we desire. But the same causes which brought about a revolution in Russia will cause uprisings in the other countries sooner or later. Certainly our situation would be better if the people all over Europe would rise and if we could talk, not with General Hoffman and Count Czernin, but with Liebknecht, Clara Zetkin, Rosa Luxemberg, and other German Socialists.[8] That we cannot do so is not our fault, and I wish to declare that we have talked to the German officials as one talks to enemies and that we have not only not lost hope, but are more convinced than ever that the peace negotiations will become a powerful weapon in the hands of the German people to fight for peace. Our voice will penetrate to the heart of the working masses, and we will obtain conditions that will make a durable peace.

"But if we are mistaken, if our call is answered only by cold silence, if propositions are made to us which are detrimental to the revolution, if the Kaiser finds the means of marching against us, then I do not know whether we have the strength to fight, but I think we have, for we will let the old tired out men return home and we will send out a cry of alarm. We will say that our honor is at stake, and we will raise a strong army of young soldiers and red guards who will fight to the last drop of blood. We certainly haven't overthrown the Czar and the bourgeoisie at home to kneel before the German Kaiser and implore for peace. But if because of economic conditions we are not able to carry on the war and must renounce our fight for the ideal, we will say to our foreign comrades that the battle for our ideals is not finished, it is merely suspended, as in 1915 when the battle against the Czar was not won, but was merely put off."[9]

This speech brought hot debate. The meeting was unlike any other I had attended. There wasn't the thrill and surge of the masses. These were harassed, determined men struggling with a gigantic problem.

Before the meeting adjourned a resolution was passed by the entire assembly. Copies of the resolution were to be distributed alike among the Central Powers and the Allies. This was it, in part:

---

[8] Max Hoffman was a German military strategist, chief of staff of the Eastern Front, and one of the negotiators at Brest-Litovsk. Count Otto von Czernin was Austro-Hungarian foreign minister during World War I.

[9] During initial peace negotiations, the Bolsheviks were hoping that allowing fraternization of troops on the front lines during the armistice would help bring German soldiers to the side of the revolution, and that members of the working class from around the world would force all of the warring countries into peace negotiations. Trotsky encouraged Lenin to drag out negotiations as long as possible to give time for this to happen. The mention of 1915 is a reference to a confrontation with the monarchy over the distribution of power that took place during a session of the Duma, which opened in July 1915, a year after Russia entered the war. Nicholas responded to calls among legislators for a more democratic government by shutting down the Duma and disregarding its calls, arguably making eventual revolution inevitable.

This meeting addresses itself to you German workers, you who are equally against the German Imperialistic acts of brigandage, as against the conquests of an imperialistic Russia. You must help us. The eyes of all are turned towards this struggle of Russia for a just and equitable peace. Will you fight to die on the Yser rather than the Vistula?[10] In the cities, in the villages, in the factories and the trenches you must engage in an active battle for peace, and prevent the imperialists from miscarrying the peace parleys.

All alone the representatives of the workers of Russia cannot bring about a general peace. You must demand that your representatives, the representatives of the workers, take part. But that is not enough. You must not be content with a peace which will reaffirm ancient injustices and forge new chains and make the weight of war fall on the shoulders of the workers. We wish a people's peace, a democratic peace, an equitable peace.

Not only Russia but all countries must send to the peace conference, not capitalists and militaristic representatives, but representatives of the masses. The reunion of all the representatives of all the Russian workers, peasants and soldiers calls to you workers of all lands, to battle for a general armistice and a general peace, a peace without annexations or indemnities, and with the right of self-determination for all people.

Long live the international revolution of the workers, peasants and soldiers.

Such a manifesto was worse than a deluge of bombs to Germany. The German officials received it smiling blandly but they never let it reach their people. They offered eagerly enough to distribute it in the land or the Allies. But the time was not yet ripe for the German Government to show the cloven hoof to Russia.[11] They wanted their delegates to reach Petrograd. So they continued their outward friendship. But each day they grew more worried. The fraternization at the front was not at all to their liking. The germ of revolution was spreading. German officers threatened to shoot their men if they talked to the Russians. Picked Germans were sent out to meet the Russians; young officers and pan-Germans who could not be corrupted.

Finally the day came for the arrival of the German delegation in Petrograd. The first delegation of sixty members with Count Kaiserling at its head was to deal with the exchange of war prisoners, and to discuss the military and naval details of an armistice.[12] They were to be merely an adjunct of the commission at Brest Litosk. The delegation was lodged at the Hotel Bristol. Straight away trouble began. The Hotel

---

[10] The Battle of the Yser took place in 1914 along the Yser River in Belgium and halted a German advance into Belgium; the Vistula is a river in Poland.

[11] To "show the cloven hoof" is to reveal a devilish purpose.

[12] Baron Kaislerling was head of the German Naval Commission, and had served in the past as naval attaché in the German embassy at Petrograd.

Bristol was an apartment hotel. Meals had to be taken at the Astoria, a hotel which had been requisitioned by the Bolshevik Government.

The Germans didn't like the arrangement. They began to order the servants about. The hotel employees were petit-bourgeoisie. They did not rebel. They received the scoldings of the Germans with trembling knees. They were completely terrorized.

The chief of the expedition, Count Kaiserling, was a close friend of Von Tirpitz.[13] Moreover he had relatives in Petrograd whom he promptly sent for. As a representative of the German Government he had lived for four years in Petrograd before the war. He had been presented to Nicholas II. He had assisted at an interview between the Czar and the Kaiser. It was at the personal request of the Kaiser that he had come to Russia.

But the Bolshevik Government had a surprise for the Germans. They had made out plans for the delegation according to German method. Each hour was arranged for, where they should go, whom they should see, what they should eat. Soldiers were stationed at the hotel and the delegation rigorously supervised. This was too much for the Germans. To escape from Germany only to be Germanized was more than they could bear. They uttered violent protests. They raised such an uproar that in the end the Bolsheviki gave in.

On the day of Count Kaiserling's arrival he was interviewed and said:

"We were told on our journey that it was dangerous to go to Petrograd, that there was famine here, but that has not prevented our coming because the German Government deemed it necessary that I myself, who have lived four years in Petrograd, should give an account of conditions here."

He was then asked about the causes of war and the prospect of revolution in Germany, and burst out:

"The Germans were forced to take up the glove which England threw down. All talk of a revolution in Germany is a lie. There is no thought of revolution. Germany is outside of politics. She abides by military regulations. I admit there is a weariness of war, and that the people struggle for peace as they have done from the beginning of the war. But we will only accept a favorable peace. We are strong. Our submarines can handle the American fleet. We do not fear America. As to the conditions in Russia we have decided not to mix in internal affairs. We do not know much about the Bolsheviki."

"But don't you know," he was asked, "that the Bolsheviki represent only one party in Russia and that there are others?"

"That," said Count Kaiserling, "does not concern me. It is a question of internal politics. We are only concerned with peace."

---

[13] Alfred Peter Friedrich von Tirpitz was a German grand admiral and had been secretary of state of the German Imperial Naval Office from 1897 to 1916. It was he who transformed Germany's navy into a world-class military force, but the navy's failures against the British led to his dismissal in 1916.

"But aren't you afraid?" he was asked, "that Bolshevism will break through the German frontier and add to the discontent that already exists in Germany?"

"Why," said Count Kaiserling with irony, "do you think Bolshevism presents a danger for us that it will not first spread to the countries of the Allies, to France and England? How little Russia knows about what is happening in Germany!"

"But you cannot deny," it was urged, "that Russia is the country nearest to Germany and that already the revolution has not been without its effect on the masses. You cannot deny there has been trouble with the navy."

"It is true," said the Count with a bored gesture, that there has been trouble on certain boats, but it was quickly suppressed. The guilty ones have already been punished. Your insinuations in general about Germany are wholly untrue. With us, all goes for the best. We enjoy full constitutional liberty. For lack of liberty England is the most abominable of all nations. Even the United States may well envy us."

It seemed useless to question the self-satisfied Count further.[14] But he was asked if he had met Trotsky.

"No," he said, "I have not had that pleasure. I have tried several times to obtain an audience. I desire to grasp him warmly by the hand, but up to the present I have not had a reply to my request."

The commissaries paid scant heed to the German delegation. The day of their arrival Zalkind, the Assistant Minister of Foreign Affairs, called at the Hotel Bristol to inquire after the health of the delegation.

When Count Kaiserling heard of this he immediately considered it an official call and set out promptly to return it.

When he arrived at Zalkind's office he explained the nature of his visit. Wheron the Assistant Minister cried out:—

"Excuse me, Count, those are ancient customs and traditions. We represent the new democracy. We do not recognize any ceremonial."

Five minutes later the discomfited Count found himself in the hall. This was only one of many surprises the Germans experienced. At times it was difficult for them to keep their temper. One member remarked: "The conditions we endure are those which would be imposed if Germany were a defeated nation." To which the Soviet, when it heard the remark, replied: "We are strong not by the force of the bayonet, but because of our revolutionary enthusiasm."

The Bolshevik officials were a great disappointment to the Germans. Count Kaiserling, after an introduction to Dybenko, the Minister of Marines, a sturdy, rough sailor with no education, exclaimed: "Is it possible that this is the Minister of Marines? He cannot speak two words. He is perhaps a brave man, but for a minister he is altogether impossible. It is the strength of the plebeian. It cannot be."

---

[14] Doty's use of passive voice here makes it unclear whether *she* was the one questioning Kaiserling, or if she received this information from another source.

Similar remarks were made of the others. Only Trotsky was considered a man of affairs. Lenine they had not met.

A few days later, the second delegation of Germans and Austrians arrived. It consisted of forty members who had come to arrange the economic relations between Russia and Germany. Count Mirbach was the head of the commission.[15] This delegation was also to lodge at the Hotel Bristol. But Count Mirbach would not hear of it. "I must have my comfort," he blustered. "To live in a hotel without a restaurant is impossible." After lengthy discussion it was agreed to accommodate the delegations at the Hotel Angleterre and the Grand Hotel.

These hotels had the best food in town. They were full of French and English. Some Frenchmen were asked to give up their rooms to the Germans. This they refused to do, so the Government requisitioned the rooms. Enraged, the entire body of French and English in both hotels left as a protest. The day the commission arrived the streets were packed. Germans had become as much a curiosity as animals in a zoo. All the entrances to the hotels were guarded. When Count Mirbach saw this he was very angry. He immediately telephoned to Trotsky and asked that the guard be withdrawn. The Count was given two rooms. Thirty automobiles were placed at the disposal of the commission. The second delegation, like the first, was familiar with Petrograd. Many of its members had lived in Russia as heads of industrial enterprises.

Shortly after arrival a conference was held at which both delegations were present. Count Mirbach presided. He opened the proceedings with a flattering eulogy of Russia. He spoke of the humanity and generosity of the Russian peace terms and said it made a new era. But the gush didn't go down with the Russians. A fiery revolutionist was promptly on his feet demanding, "What about German humanity? Why are you arresting Socialists?" For a moment the Count was unnerved. Then his arrogance came to the rescue. With a superior air he said stiffly: "We cannot deal with civil affairs here. Our business is confined to technicalities. Besides, the arrests alluded to are probably rumors." It was a lively session. The hottest debate centered about the right of the delegation to freedom of action. The Russians rubbed it in that they were treated like prisoners at Brest Litosk. But the Bolshevik Government, unlike the German, had nothing to conceal from its people. It agreed to give the commission liberty on condition that its members did not enter into private business enterprises.

One day I went to the Grand Hotel for lunch. I was curious to see the Germans. The leaders of the delegations were not in the main dining-room, but the secretaries and under attachés sat at a long table. They were lean and hungry looking. There wasn't a fat German among them. There were no protruding stomachs. They wore

---

[15] Wilhelm Graf von Mirbach-Harff was a German diplomat who had served as the embassy clerk in St. Petersburg from 1908 to 1911; after participating in the negotiations at Brest-Litovsk, he became German ambassador to Russia in April 1918. He was assassinated in July 1918 in Moscow by a Left SR who was trying to foment war between Germany and Russia in a move that marked the beginning of the Left SR revolt in Moscow.

frock coats and were stiff and serious. They were like wooden images beside the tempestuous, passionate, vigorous Russian. There was chicken and rice for lunch, with a thick, rich sauce. I remembered the scanty and greaseless boiled food of Germany in 1916. The Germans also remembered it. They did everything but lick their plates. They couldn't get enough. They kept ordering more. Once some official came into the room and the men at the long table rose stiffly, heels together and hand to head. It was so unlike the Russians, who lolled in chairs, cigarette in mouth, called each other Tavarish (comrade) and spoke with passion.

The Sunday after the arrival of the delegates, a peace parade was ordered. It was a demonstration of the power of the Bolsheviki. The Soviet asked the populace to turn out. As early as ten o'clock the streets swarmed with people, when I reached the Nevsky, which is twice as broad as Fifth Avenue, a solid mass of people reaching from curb to curb were pouring through it. Once caught in the crowd, it was impossible to get out. I was swept along with the surging mass. They were all working people, women with shawls over their heads and men in shabby clothes. There were many companies of soldiers, sailors, and even Cossacks. Not less than sixty or seventy thousand were in line. Sometimes this mass joined hands and sang, sometimes they talked. They were never still. They breathed emotion, passion, rebellion. They were like a great on-rushing river. To stop them was like trying to stop Niagara. It could not be done. If some were hewn down or pushed aside, the stream would still flow on. These were some of the inscriptions on the banners borne in the processions: "Long live the Revolution of the Workers." "Down with international Imperialism." "Long live a general democratic peace." "Long live the power of the Soviet." "Fight without mercy against the Saboteurs." "Down with the conciliators." "Long live the liberty and fraternity of the Russian people." "The Constituent Assembly must recognize the power of the Soviets." "The Kadets are enemies of the people." "The enemies of the people must not have a place in the Constituent Assembly." "Malediction to all people who sabotage the Revolution." "Long live the union fraternal of workers, peasants, sailors, soldiers and Cossacks."

The German delegation had been taken to rooms on the Nevsky Prospect. From the windows they could look down on this surging mob. There must have been panic in their hearts. It was what the People's Commissaries had counted on. They wanted the Germans to see the strength of the people. It had its effect, but an effect far from helpful. The Germans were more determined than ever to prevent the spread of revolution. That glimpse from the window had revealed what an uprising in Germany would mean. The delegation saw themselves mercilessly shot down. Orders immediately went forth to keep all Russian news from Germany. In violation of their agreement fraternization at the front was stopped and the Russian soldiers were given cognac and vodka in exchange for bread. Everything was done to spread disorder and drunkenness. German propaganda flooded the land. Russian soldiers were told to hurry home, that the land was being distributed and they wouldn't get their share.

But the Soviets worked steadily on. They made desperate efforts to get the revolutionary news into Germany. Printing presses were set up at any odd spot. Soldiers lugged tons of literature on their backs to the front. It was dropped by aeroplane into the trenches.

The Russian Soviet began to get out a daily paper in German. It was called Die Fakel. It was a passionate appeal to "Our brother German Socialits to join in the Revolution." Such talk was fatal to Germany. It must be stopped at all costs. A great wagon load of Die Fakel was seized at the front by the Germans, and the wagon and papers burned. This enraged the Russians. There was an indignation meeting at Smolny Institute. But the peace negotiations were going forward favorably at Brest Litosk. The Russians did not wish to impede them.

The peace negotiations at Brest Litosk had opened with all the pomp and formality the Germans could command. Prince Leopold of Bavaria had opened the proceedings. The Turkish Ambassador made an address of welcome in which he said, "I salute the Russian delegates who had the courage in the face of the whole world to talk of peace in the interests of humanity."

Next it was Von Kuhlmann who was saying sweet nothings.[16] He remarked, "It is a great honor for the country which I represent to meet with the Russian delegates and put an end to war. The conference will work out in smallest detail the basis and conditions on which pacific and friendly relations can be renewed, particularly in the cultural and economic life, and will deliberate on the best way to heal the wounds of war. Our conference will be full of the spirit of humanity and mutual esteem. But to be on firm ground we must consider the events of history, as well as the new principles which we are here to discuss."

Even this opening speech had its little back fling. That allusion to the "events of history" boded ill. There was an arrière pensée to all the Germans said.[17] They were trying to get everything and give nothing. When it was seen that the Allies would not join in the negotiations, and that the Ukraine and Finland had split from Russia, the Germans grew haughty and superior. Still they continued to negotiate. It was imperative they have peace with Russia. They wanted to send their soldiers to the western front. But the Russian delegates saw what they were after. Said Kameneff:

"I can say frankly that to arrive at a separate peace the German generals are willing to make large concessions. But that is not what we have in mind. We went to Brest Litosk with the conviction that our words would pass over the heads of the Ger-

---

[16] Richard von Kühlmann, an industrialist and diplomat, served as Germany's secretary of state for foreign affairs during the peace negotiations with Russia. He had worked actively to help the Bolsheviks come to power so that the instability they created could be exploited to achieve peace on terms favorable to Germany.

[17] An *arrière pensée* is a concealed notion.

man Generals to the people; that our words would enable the people to take the guns from the Generals, by means of which they are now being led around by the nose."

But the hope of a revolution in Germany daily grew less. The German press abounded in stories of the chaos in Russia. Russia was said to be falling to pieces from riots and bloodshed, that no man's life was safe.

Along with this picture of a broken Russia went the tale of the secret treaties. The secret treaties were published broadcast. It was pointed out that the Allies had aggressive designs, that England meant to take Persia, France possessions in Asia Minor, and Italy towns of Austria. The German Government used this evidence to intimidate their people. Said the press:

"Beware of revolution; if there is revolution in Germany the country will become like Russia, a prey to the whole world. The Allies will seize upon the Fatherland and divide the spoils."

Fear entered into the hearts of the people. Strikes died down. Once more the Germans rallied to their flag. When the officials saw this they breathed again. They took new life. They grew domineering. They began to flirt with Finland, Courland, and the Ukraine, and bring them under the German sway. The Ukraine Rada, after having taken large sums of money from France, sold out to Germany.[18] Only the Russian workers, the Bolsheviki in the Ukraine, fought desperately against the intruders. In Finland and Courland it was the same. The whole upper stratum of society in both countries was German. They held out welcoming hands to the conquerors. When the Russian Soviet realized what had happened, they were enraged. They expressed themselves in no gentle terms. But the Germans only smiled sweetly and said:

"We are not annexing territory. We are merely giving the people of Finland and the Ukraine aid; as to Courland, Poland and Lithuania, they want us to govern them. They have called and we have answered."

When events reached this stage a great indignation meeting was held at Smolny Institute. I went to the meeting. The excitement was tremendous.

Kameneff had come back from Brest Litosk to make his report. In conclusion he said: "Our discussion rests on Poland, Courland, and Lithuania. Shall they be given the right of self-government without intervention of German bayonets. They must be. We will not give in on this point. We will have peace, but I repeat it is not at the moment to be found in the pocket of any of us. Be firm and have faith in our cause; in time that will bring peace, but when, no one can say."

That night affairs looked black for the Germans. The members of the Soviet were stirred to a frenzy. Through the dense tobacco smoke men kept springing to their feet and hurling oaths at the Germans. The majority of the Assembly wanted

---

[18] The Verkhovna Rada, sometimes just called the Rada, is the parliament of Ukraine. Although the Rada agreed to German support in granting protection to Ukraine against the Bolsheviks, within a short time the Germans came to be seen as occupiers, and Ukrainian allegiances shifted toward the Bolsheviks.

to arm and fight. A volunteer army of men, fighting for freedom, should go out and annihilate the despots. But then came reports on the state of the Russian army.

In some places there were no shoes, in others no food. Everywhere transportation had broken down. The Assembly grew desperate. Men faced each other grimly. Finally one man sprang to his feet and suggested that at least the German delegation could be given a lesson. Those men were in their power. Why not proceed to their hotel and take the delegates out, one by one, and cut their throats and drop them into the canal? This suggestion caused no horror. It was even applauded. A little more and the Assembly would have acted on it. For a moment the fate of the German delegation hung by a thread. It is small wonder that Count Mirbach has since been murdered. The only wonder is that the deed was not done before.

Hourly the tension between Germany and Russia grew greater. But the Russians believed themselves helpless. They had no army, no equipment, no longer a front. They signed the German peace proposals. If the Bolsheviki fail, it will be because they made this fatal mistake. Representatives of great ideals can never compromise. The seriousness of what they were doing they knew well. Said Trotsky:

"History will say we dealt with capitalists while our comrades in Germany, the independent socialists, were arrested. Our only moral excuse is that we are arresting the capitalists in this country. We showed the German bourgeoisie their fellow Russian bourgeoisie in prison, but they made no protest. If we treat with German bourgeoisie it is as strikers deal with their employer. We act as though this were the final peace parley, but the time will come when we will talk to Liebknecht at the head of a revolutionary Germany. I am sure if the Russian bourgeoisie were in power they would make a shameful peace with Germany in order to strengthen their power at home. But we are stronger really than any other country, because the soldiers are with the government."

So do all politicians argue. Evil is done that good may come. But an idealist cannot so reason. He must die for his cause, even as Christ was crucified.

This compromise with Germany, the suppression of the press, the arrest of moderate socialists, and like intolerant acts were causing dissension among the Bolsheviki. It was making a break that may prove fatal to revolutionary Russia. Said one Russian in answer to Trotsky's speech: "Cure yourself. You denounce the arrest of German socialists, but we hear today that Chernov, once a representative of this Soviet, has been arrested. Such acts provoke greater indignation than the arrest of Liebknecht." At this point the speaker was silenced. He was yelled down by cries or fury. But he had laid bare a weak spot.

The idealist must preach ideals with clean hands. Nor would a failure to sign the peace terms have left Russia any worse off.[19] Germany could have done little more than she has done. She might have marched to Petrograd and taken possession, but

---

[19] This point is debatable; certainly Lenin felt he had no choice but to accept German terms.

beyond that she could not have gone. Russia and Siberia together are as big as all Europe and the United States. To conquer such a territory Germany would have had to move all her troops from the western front. She could handle the west or she could handle the east, but she could not handle both together. If a small army of Germans had attempted to invade Russia, they would merely have had their throats cut and been dropped into the canal. Had the Russians had the faith to refuse to sign undemocratic peace terms, the war might have been over today. But however much we may regret this failure of the Bolsheviki to hold to their ideal, it is not for us to judge. Let us turn our eyes to the future. Let us recognize the power of the Russian workers. If they were not strong, Germany would not have treated with them. That Germany recognized the Soviets meant that in January, 1918, the mass of the people were behind the Soviets.

Whatever we think about the Bolsheviki, whether we believe them all good or all bad, we must let them work out their own salvation. We have expressed our faith in a new creed. We believe in self-government. We believe in it even for convicts. Surely then we ought to believe in it for the Bolsheviki. Little by little Russia will right itself. Given freedom and a chance to breathe and she will stabilize and grow strong. Beside a strong, free Russia, imperialistic Germany cannot stand. It is not Germany that will conquer Russia, it is Russia that will revolutionize Germany.

Chapter VIII
THE WOMEN OF RUSSIA—THE WOMAN COMRADE

To study the woman's movement in the midst of a revolution was difficult, particularly difficult in Russia, where there is no feminist group. For Russian women do not stand out as women. They have not struggled for their own emancipation.[1] Their light has been the man's fight, their life the man's life. They have endured years of exile in Siberia. They have fought for the revolution.

They are good comrades. It is here the woman's strength lies. Her own needs and the child's have been subordinated. The home, the child, the school, the vote, social welfare, to these things—except in individual cases—she has not devoted herself. She is not a good housewife. There is no regularity in the home. Meals are never on time. It is difficult to discover when a Russian family doesn't eat. I visited one family at eleven, at two, at four, at six, at eight, and they were always at the table. If they weren't eating, they were drinking tea. Over the steaming samovar the men and women discussed the affairs of the universe. In the country as in the city woman is man's mate. The peasant woman works in the fields. The farmer views her work with respect. The Russian woman is a man in petticoats.

She hasn't given her life to personal service and social welfare, but to man's fight for political freedom. This life with man has made her frank and natural. She is quick to understand and full of energy. Her endurance is marvelous.

Early in November, 1917, the workingmen and soldiers, the Bolsheviki, captured the government. But this did not change the position of women. They were as much in evidence as ever. The streets were packed with soldiers and with women with shawls over their heads. Even the wealthy women wore shawls and aprons, to

---

[1] Doty is not entirely accurate in this claim, and Doty's own brand of feminist activism probably limited her ability to see Russian women's activism on its own terms: as Rochelle Ruthchild has demonstrated, Russia had feminist organizations going back to 1904. However, these organizations did not use the term "feminism," instead phrasing their demands in terms of other Russian movements, most often referring to the "woman question" rather than feminism. Even so, the Russian Revolution was partly a product of women's activism, as food riots during an International Women's Day celebration set off the February Revolution. Furthermore, although Russian organizations emphasized "equal rights" rather than feminism, women were major figures in Russian revolutionary movements and gender issues were important to the revolutionary ethos.

hide their identity. Petrograd became a city of working people. There were no private sleighs or Parisian costumes, and the few automobiles were used by the workingmen of the Bolshevik government. The women trudged through the snow. They asked no favors. They jumped on and off street-cars while they were in motion. They fought for a foothold on a car step and clutched a soldier's arm to keep from falling. They were good-humored and unafraid.

It was they who kept the city going. In blinding snowstorms they shoveled snow off the car tracks and tended the switches. The thermometer was twenty degrees below zero, it was light only from nine to three, but in the biting cold and stinging storm the women worked hour after hour. They were indomitable.

When a feminist movement does arise, nothing can stop such women. What they can do has been shown on one or two occasions. In the first days of the Revolution, when Kerensky and the Provisional Government were in power, the question of woman suffrage arose. Did the program of the government include votes for women? The Constituent Assembly was to be elected on the basis of universal suffrage. Did that mean women? The Russian women believed it did. It never entered their minds that men might betray them; they were men's comrades and equals. But when the question was asked, the men were silent. A terrible doubt crept into the women's hearts. It was not to be borne. All over Russia there was a spontaneous uprising. The All Russian League of Women's Enfranchisement, which corresponds to our American suffrage organization of which Mrs. Carrie Chapman Catt is president, was swamped. Women poured into the offices night and day. Meetings were held, and a great manifestation was organized. In March, 1917, 40,000 women marched to the Tauride Palace where the Provisional Government sat.[2] At the head of the procession rode women on horseback. They kept the way clear and acted as police. Behind them on foot was the great women's army. In their midst, in an automobile, rode Vera Figner, a woman who had spent twenty years in Siberian exile.[3] The spectators went wild with enthusiasm. They threw flowers at Vera Figner and urged the women on.

At the palace a delegation entered to interview the president and vice-president of the Council of Workingmen and Soldiers' Deputies. These gentlemen said they must confer with their committees. They talked and argued long, but the women outside the palace never moved. At last the vice-president appeared and said, "For your just demand we will struggle." But this did not satisfy the women.

---

[2] This point alone would seem to contradict Doty's claim that there was no feminist movement in Russia.

[3] Vera Figner, a child of the Russian nobility (like many female revolutionaries) was a leader of the People's Will, a terrorist group that planned the successful assassination of Tsar Alexander II in 1881. She was arrested and sentenced to death, but her sentence was commuted, and she lived in exile before spending about a decade abroad, returning to Russia in 1915. She became a hero in Russia and was also legendary in the United States.

They demanded that the president of the Council address them. Again there was a long wait. Still the women did not move. Their patience was extraordinary. The manifestation had begun at 10 A. M. It was now late afternoon. Pools of water stood in the street. The women were wet and hungry, but they would not disperse. At length the president appeared. Then Mrs. Shishkina Yavein, the president of the Woman Suffrage League, made a speech which ended with these words:[4]

"Women have been the faithful comrades of men in their gigantic struggle for Russian freedom. Women have gone to prison and marched to the gallows. The best of us, like Vera Figner, have looked into the eyes of death without fear. We are convinced of our right to equality in the new, free Russia, for the creation of which we have given our all. You have said the Constituent Assembly shall be convoked on the basis of universal suffrage. We hope and believe this means women as well as men, but the experience of our western sisters has shown that men have used the word 'universal' as applying only to one-half of the population, themselves, and have classed women with criminals, idiots, and children. Therefore we have come on behalf of the Russian women to demand that the word 'universal' shall be interpreted to include women, and that the Constituent Assembly shall be elected by the will of the whole people and not by half of it. We will not leave this place until we have received the answer that women as well as men shall have the right to vote in the Constituent Assembly."

The president of the Council of Workingmen and Soldiers saw that he was beaten, and capitulated. He assured the women that he was with them and advised that a delegation be sent to Prince Lvoff, the then president of the Council of Ministers. This was done, and still the patient crowd in the street waited. But victory came in the end. Prince Lvoff formally declared that universal suffrage meant women as well as men.

On March 19, 1917, political freedom was granted Russian women, but as soon as the battle was won, Russian women flowed back into the general life.

They did not stay together as women; they merged their entity with that of the men. When the Bolshevik Revolution came, some women were for it and some against it. The cleavage was that of the men. The wealthy women, the intellectuals, the bourgeoisie, sided with Kerensky and the Provisional Government; the peasant women and factory workers were with the Bolsheviki.

When I reached Petrograd it was a city of peasants and workers. Even the intellectuals were in hiding. Catherine Breshkovskaya, "The Little Grandmother of the Revolution," who had spent so many years in exile, was not to be found. It was said she feared imprisonment. The women who came to the Bolshevik meetings were peasants and factory workers. They were straight, slender creatures with short hair,

---

[4] Poliksena Shishkina-Yavein, a St. Petersburg physician, was head of the All-Russian League for Women's Equality and had also campaigned for the abolition of state-licensed brothels.

boyish manners, and burning eyes. They rarely rose to speak. They were at ease with the men, but they let them be spokesmen.

Only one government position was given to a woman—Madam Kollontai was made Minister of Social Welfare. She is the first woman minister the world has had.[5] I interviewed her one day. There is nothing radical in her appearance. She is slender, with light hair and blue eyes, a cross between a school teacher and an English woman of birth. Yet she has spent nine years in exile and for twenty years has been a revolutionist. We were soon in hot debate.

"Why," I asked her, "when women have the same rights as men, are so few coming to the front?"

She paused before answering and then said: "Women are shy. They don't yet want public positions."

"Perhaps," I suggested, "there aren't so many Bolshevik women as men. Perhaps women are more conservative."[6]

Quick as a flash came her reply: "No, that isn't true. Women who earn their living are as radical as men. It's only the women who stay at home, the mothers, who are conservative."

"And what work are you doing?" I asked.

She frowned and sighed, and then said: "Very little yet. I'm having great difficulty. The clerks in my department are employees of the old regime. They won't recognize me. I can't make them obey. I want to open up children's institutions and look after the orphans, but it will take time."

"Why," I asked, "do you believe in a dictatorship of the working people? You didn't believe in a dictatorship of the Czar?"

She flushed and then said quickly: "I don't believe in a dictatorship; I believe in a representative government. I want the Constituent Assembly called. But meantime the Bolsheviki have to be dictators. Really, you know," she added earnestly, "the people are much more violent than the leaders. The people are angry; you cannot hold them in check."

After my interview with Madam Kollontai I tried to get in touch with Marie Spiradonova, the other Bolshevik woman who stands out in great prominence. She is adored by the peasants. She is a tiny slip of a person probably not more than five feet tall. She wears her hair in a braid bound tightly about her head. She is pale, with

---

[5] In fact, as Doty herself acknowledges, Kollontai replaced another female minister of social welfare, Countess Panina. Alexandra Kollontai was the most prominent Bolshevik feminist; she became a controversial figure among the Bolsheviks because of her feminism and free attitudes about sex. She was made a foreign ambassador, serving in Norway and Mexico, arguably to get her out of the way.

[6] It is not surprising that Kollontai would be angered by this suggestion, as the notion that women were naturally conservative was a common perception in Russia, and one that Kollontai was actively fighting.

great circles under her eyes. Under the Czar she was horribly abused. She was a revolutionist and killed the Lieutenant-Governor of a province, who was flogging and brutally ill-treating the peasants. For this she was imprisoned for years and finally exiled to Siberia for life. During her imprisonment she was abused by the keepers. Her body was beaten with sticks and burned with the soldiers' lighted cigarettes. Today she is hardly more than a wraith, but her power over the peasants is enormous. As she stands before them on the platform at their great meetings, she can stir the sturdy peasant to a frenzy of passion with a sweep of her hand, or quiet him as though he were a child.

I met Spiradonova at Smolny Institute and stopped her for a talk. I asked her the same questions I had asked Madam Kollontai.

"Women," said she, "are as great idealists as men. The reason more Bolshevik women aren't prominent is because they haven't the strength or the training and they aren't practical. But it will come one day; there will be no difference between men and women."[7]

The Russian woman has courage. It makes no difference in what grade of life she may be. Whether a peasant or a countess, a factory worker or an intellectual, she is a fighter.

I met a very wealthy woman who had been a Red Cross nurse. In the early days of the war many of the women of means became nurses. To be a Red Cross nurse in Russia is a dangerous business. Unlike other countries, the Russians often put their hospitals directly at the front. This woman had lived in a dugout. Many of the nurses lived in dugouts. Daily they were exposed to death. One day a shell struck the dugout in which this woman and eight other nurses were. Seven were instantly killed. This woman was bitter against the Bolsheviki. She felt her country was going to ruin.

A wealthy woman who was caught in the Bolshevik machine was the Countess Panin. It was through her inspiration that Noradny Dome was built, an amusement resort for the people. The entrance fee in January, 1918, was half a rouble, about twelve cents, the cost of admission to the theater and opera-house comparatively small. While a place of amusement, it is also a place of education. The best that Russia has to give the people, the plays of Tolstoy and Gorky, are acted in the theater. During the days of Kerensky and the Provisional Government the Countess Panin was made an assistant minister in the government relief work. While in office she raised 92,000 roubles for her work. When the Bolsheviki came into power the Countess was deposed and the money demanded. But the Countess refused to surrender the money. She said she held it in trust for the people and that the Bolsheviki didn't repre-

---

[7] Bryant asked Spirodonova (Doty is inconsistent in her spelling of the name, but typically the name is transliterated as Spiridonova) essentially the same question, and got a somewhat different reply: she implied in this instance that women are more principled than men, and thus less fit to be politicians (who are, by definition, not particularly principled). Bryant also said that Angelica Balabanov, another revolutionist, told her basically the same thing.

sent the people. One day soldiers appeared at the Countess's house. She was arrested and led to the grim old fortress of Peter and Paul.

While I was in Petrograd the Countess Panin was tried.[8] In the Nicholai Palace, before a solemn row of workingmen, appeared the Countess, delicate, gentle, modest, but unafraid. The judge who sat in the middle acted as president and opened the proceedings.

The Countess Panin was charged with sabotage. In retaining the ninety-two thousand roubles she was accused of impeding the work of the Bolshevik government. The Countess denied her guilt. Her lawyer in defending her said: "As judges, the Tribunal must be impartial. Forget party differences and the class struggle. Say to yourselves it is not the Countess Panin who appears before us, but Citizen Panin, who has consecrated her life to the service of the people. Judge her according to your conscience, and remember you have before you a woman who has given her all to the people." When the lawyer ceased speaking an old man among the spectators staggered to his feet. He uttered a despairing cry: "I can bear no more, I can bear no more. How can one judge such a woman?" Then he fell fainting to the floor and was borne from the room. He proved to be the old director of Noradny Dome, the People's House founded by the Countess.

It was some minutes before the court-room settled down. When order was restored a workingman from a munitions factory arose. "Comrades," he said, "I come not to defend the Countess Panin, whom I do not know, but the benefactress known to all Petrograd, to all Russia, to all Europe. There are many countesses and duchesses, but only one has held out her hand to the people. She has gone among the workers without disgust at the smoke and dirt; she has brought to the workers instruction. The workers' children find in her a mother. The Countess is not a traitor to the people; she is not a counter-revolutionary. I pray you judge her as a citizen. The eyes of the world are upon you. It must not be said the Revolutionary Tribunal is a wild beast which hurls itself upon its first victim. We shall be criminals if in the person of the Countess we take revenge on the class to which she belongs."

There was a mad burst of applause. But instantly another workman sprang to his feet. His words came hot and fast: "Beloved comrades, the people must sweep aside all that blocks their way. Do not let yourself be moved by the generosity of the Countess, but judge her as she deserves. Much has been said of her generosity, but bandits can be generous. Do not let hysterical cries trouble you when the future of the working class is at stake. Judge the Countess as one who by her acts wishes to make the people rise against the new government. Countess, what have you done with the ninety-two thousand roubles?"

---

[8] Though imprisoned for refusing to return the money, she was later released with the understanding that she would return the money when the Constituent Assembly met—which, of course, did not happen.

The Countess had grown white; her lips were pressed together, but when the man sat down, she arose: "I think it is the soldiers who will best understand me. Like a sentinel I cannot abandon without proper authorization what was given me to defend. I cannot abandon the money of the people. It was the people who placed me in the ministry of public welfare, and it is to the people I will give back the money. I will render it to the Constituent Assembly on the first day that that body meets, but not to the Bolshevik Government."

Still white and trembling, the Countess sat down. Then the judges withdrew. They were absent a long time. When they returned, the president arose and pronounced sentence: "We sentence," he said, "the Countess to the Fortress of Peter and Paul until she delivers over the ninety-two thousand roubles to the Bolshevik Government."

Such was the fate of the Countess. But feeling ran high about her imprisonment. Before I left Petrograd she had been released on bail on condition that she deliver the ninety-two thousand roubles to the Constituent Assembly the first day it met.

Whatever Russia's future, in it women will play a big part. Under the old regime they had little chance to express themselves. They gave themselves wholly to the fight for the revolution. They accepted man's methods. They forsook the things nearest their hearts, and when the Bolshevik Revolution came, the working women flung themselves into it. Again they accepted man's methods. But what was needed was the woman's spirit; the mother half of the race preaching tolerance and love.

Had that element been powerful the Bolsheviki might not have gone on the rocks. The mothers would have been in the forefront of the working class movement clamoring for the child of the future. They would have fought against imprisonment, brutality, suppression of the press, and all the old evils of capitalism.

Undemocratic peace terms would not have been signed if the chief purpose of men and women alike had been to make a decent world for the child to come. And if the man insisted that these things could only come through force, then was the time for the woman to show that only force based on love has value. When the man said for this we must fight, let the woman whisper, yes, for this you must give your life, but you must not take. For beauty is founded on beauty and right upon right, and real democracy springs from a free and enlightened people and is not achieved by dictatorship.

Chapter IX
HEADING TOWARD HOME

How to get out of Russia, that was the question. My passport had to be vised by the Bolsheviki and the British military authorities. It was like mixing oil and water. Who to go to first? I decided on the Bolsheviki. My career as an Amerikanski Bolshevik Tavarish (an American Bolshevik Comrade) was satisfactory. The long line of visé seekers was pushed aside. My passport was quickly stamped, but then, oh, then! I asked to carry out papers. "Certainly," said the amiable Bolshevik Foreign Office. "We'll make you a Russian courier. You can take what you like."

I tried to smile appreciation, but my heart sank. What would the British say? I hurried around to their office. "Of course," I said, "I won't be a courier if you don't want me to. But," I added, smiling, "it's only as far as Sweden and between there and England you can search me as much as you like."

He was a friendly English captain and he saw my point. "I suppose," he said, smiling, "if you weren't the courier some real Russian Bolshevik would be, and of the two you're probably the least harmful." So I tucked my package of papers covered with many red seals into my bag and made ready.

It had taken a whole week to get the visés. Besides the British and the Russian, I had to go to the American, French, Swedish and Norwegian embassies.[1] It meant waiting hours in dingy rooms among struggling and desperate people. Often I felt I should have preferred the front line trenches.

Each year the regulations grow worse. A correspondent's life is particularly pitiful. He is always suspected. It has become a religion to suspect correspondents, so I take pride in my passport. Each visé indicates good conduct or clever strategy.

The train for Sweden left at 8:40 A. M. There are no short cuts from Russia these days. One couldn't go to Helsingfors and thence by boat to Stockholm. Instead, one had to go to the northern-most corner of Finland, cross a river and then down the length of Sweden. It was a journey which took five days and nights from Petrograd.

I left in a driving snowstorm. At 8:40 A. M. it was still black night. At such an hour it was like hunting for a needle in a haystack to find a sleigh, but at last I secured one. I was thankful I had no trunk, only two bags and a carryall. The sleigh was

---

[1] Doty visited all of these countries on her way home, but most of her discussion of those visits has been edited out of this edition.

open. I was beaten and buffeted by the storm. The snow drifted down my neck and up my sleeves. At home we would never have ventured out in such a gale. It would have been called a blizzard. The thermometer was 20 degrees below zero, but in war time one cannot bother about trifles. Conditions must be accepted and you either live or die. The train was two hours late in starting. A snowplow went ahead to clear the track. Two hours after we left we were out of Russia and in Finland. At once I began to notice a difference. Things began to be orderly.[2] A dining car was put on. The food was scanty but well served. I felt of the white tablecloth and napkins with exquisite pleasure. It was so long since I had seen clean linen. The Bolsheviki do not need capitalistic luxury. But the waiter troubled me. He was servile and hung around for tips. I preferred the self-respecting Bolshevik brand. But we didn't keep our dining car long. Even in countries where there is neither a revolution nor a war, railroad travel is slipping back to the discomforts of the Middle Ages.

At night we stopped at a railroad station for dinner. We were allowed fifteen minutes. At these eating places the food is put on a long table. You buy a ticket and help yourself. That is, you help yourself if you can. The men on the train rushed the dining-room. They were as thick as flies. You saw no table, only backs and legs. It was tantalizing. There was no slipping a head or arm in anywhere. At every meal throughout the journey it was the same. I should have died of starvation before I reached Stockholm if it hadn't been for a young American Y.M.C.A. man. He must have been a football player before he joined the Y.M.C.A. He was six feet tall and had a mighty muscle. Brute force and tips won. He and I always got food. The next day we were many hours late.

We arrived at eating stations at ungodly hours, ten, four, and six. Outside, the storm still raged. We reached the end of Finland late at night, too late to cross to Sweden. Our train pulled up on a siding and there it stayed. That night there were no sheets, but we were given a blanket. I had become hardened to sleeping in my clothes. I needed them for warmth. I rolled up tight in the blanket.

In the morning we were still on the siding. By nine it was light. At ten the hungry men were fuming for their breakfast, but we were in the middle of snowbanks. An engine house was the only visible building. The thermometer stood at 40 degrees below zero. But the Y.M.C.A. man appeared, radiant and smiling. "I have a plan. Come along. We'll get breakfast." He tried to open the train door, but it was locked. We were prisoners until we reached the station and our passport had been examined. But my companion was dauntless. He made for the last car. The door to the rear platform was open. We climbed up over the rail and jumped into the snow. Then we ran to the engine house. Inside we found the engineer. Several kroners produced the desired effect. He oiled up and the Y.M.C.A. man helped me on to the engine. I sat beside the

---

[2] A wave of relief at things seeming clean and orderly after Russia is a common trope in travel narratives.

engine driver and he pulled the whistle. With a puff-puff we moved out of the building. It was a joyous but chilly mile ride to the station. We bumped into a freight car on the way and took it along. We had a great breakfast and three cups of coffee, the first coffee in many a day. We were very superior when the other passengers arrived.

All morning we wrestled with the Finnish authorities. When we had been examined and passed, we collected our luggage and got a sleigh. Torneo, Finland, is, I imagine, like some town in Alaska. It consists of a vast stretch of snow, a few wooden buildings and a church. The Finnish sleighs are like beds. There is no seat except for the driver. The bed part is covered with straw. On this you lie, three in a row, covered by a great fur rug. It is the only way to keep from freezing. By this time the temperature was 50 degrees below zero. As we sped along I peered out from the fur rug. My eyebrows were instantly white with frost. We were crossing the frozen river which separates Finland from Sweden. There was nothing to see but a flat white world.

At the Swedish border we filed into a long wooden building. Here we encountered a surprise. In Russia and the Anglo-Saxon countries you are examined for dangerous literature. But Sweden is chiefly concerned with the body. She is like Germany. We were shown into a speckless room with an operating table and a doctor and nurse in white. After a hunt for germs we were passed on. Modern science in a snow wilderness seemed queer. System and order had descended upon us. But in Sweden, like Germany, if the orders get mixed things go wrong.

Our berth reservations were for the preceding night. The Finnish train had missed connections. We found we were berthless. Tips and the Y.M.C.A. man got me a place, but the majority of the passengers had to sit up for three days and two nights. Among our number was an English family fleeing from Russia, a young mother with three children under six. They had no nurse. Their Russian nurse had been a Bolshevik and refused to accompany them. Besides this family there was a middle aged French woman, frightfully ill. She wished to die in her native land. The journey brought on horrible paroxysms of pain. All the afternoon and evening we waited for trains. We were crowded together in a dingy waiting-room. The time was spent ministering to the sick woman or consoling a child who had fallen from a bench. There is a law in Sweden that the car temperature must be 60 before the train is allowed to start. But fuel these days is scarce. The wood was green. The heat would not increase. The train was scheduled to leave at 7 P.M. It was one before we were permitted to get on board. The wooden benches in the waiting-room had grown unbearable. The sick woman moaned with pain. I dropped into my berth exhausted. The Swedish train was beautifully equipped. It was as perfect as any Pullman. Gone were the days of Russian fleas and dirt. But at six in the morning we were awakened by great excitement. The sick woman was dying. A doctor was demanded. This woman was in the car next to mine.

In the night the steam pipes in that car burst. For hours the passengers had been without any heat. We were all ordered to get up. The thermometer in our car was only 40, but we were ordered to take in the passengers of the other car. There weren't enough seats to go round. Most of the day I stood in the swaying aisle of the train. That night the heat in our car gave out. Before we reached Stockholm the heating system of every car, including the baggage car, had broken down from the cold. We had to take on a whole new set of cars. The constant delays made the food problem difficult. We arrived at stations at the wrong hours. One night we had dinner at six and then nothing to eat until three the next day. But everything comes to an end. On the fifth day at one in the morning we reached Stockholm....

When we stepped out of the station we were in the middle of the beautiful city. It lay there rigid and still under the shining stars. There was not a sound nor a human being visible. Gone are the days of taxis and sleighs. Horses and petrol have given out. The tram cars had stopped for the night. Finally a hotel porter appeared with a hand sled. He piled our bags upon it and we trudged off in the hard, glistening snow. Stockholm is crowded these days with refugees from Russia and Germany. It was hard to get rooms. But ten of us found accommodations at the Strand Hotel.

The next morning when I woke it was some moments before I realized where I was. Then I lay and exulted. The bed was so soft; the sheets smelled so sweet; the room was so clean. It was marvelous to have a telephone that worked; an electric light that turned on; a bell that brought a smiling maid in white cap and apron. I felt like ragged Cinderella turned into a princess. No longer should I have to sleep in my clothes; go without baths; be covered with fleas, and hear rifle shots and machine guns in the street below. Turbulent Russia was a thing of the past.

I had my breakfast in bed. For twenty-four hours I reveled in peace, beauty, and order. Then I began to look beneath the surface. On the street life was so still. Every one dressed alike. The men wore frock coats and high silk hats. They were pompous and funny, like wooden images. Their faces were set or smiled blandly. What was the matter? Weren't they alive? Had passion died out? I grew hungry for the dirty Bolsheviki. They could think and talk. They were not made in a mold. I missed the crowd; the passionate street corner arguments; the pulsating life. Was there no happy medium? Couldn't one be clean and orderly and yet alive? Mightn't physical things be systematized but the human soul left free?...

It was time to go.... As the train chugged along I had much time for thought. There was no light to read by, for there was no fuel. One solitary candle illumined the car. I snuggled down in my corner and in the flickering candlelight while the train rushed on through the snow-covered country I thought and thought....

At nine o'clock I got out to change cars. The train that was to take me from Sweden to Norway was due at midnight. But 12 o'clock came and went, and no train. I sat in the little waiting-room with two or three men and women who snored peacefully in their hard chairs. The minutes rolled by. Each bulletin made the train later. It was 3:30 A.M. before it arrived. I tumbled into my berth, tired and spent. But somehow physical comforts had ceased to matter. I was still filled with dreams of the future. I seemed to see women the world around joining hands to meet the new day that had dawned.

I had reached Norway. Two-thirds of my journey around the world was over. But the danger was not past. To reach England I had to cross the North Sea. Submarines filled those waters. Daily the papers told of ships sunk. Germans filled the land. They poured into Denmark, ate up the food, and drifted to Norway. They bought Norwegian hotels under a Swedish name. Weary Russians and English and Americans homeward bound lived at these hotels and discussed their woes. The bland proprietor listened and reported to the German Government. The Germans knew when the boat left for England. The English kept the date of sailing a secret. The passengers were in darkness. But the Germans sat on the seashore and watched proceedings. It was very disconcerting. The sense of danger and intrigue was nerve-racking....

The English boats are small and the North Sea very rough. When we got out of the fjord we began to toss like an eggshell. I had crossed the ocean without seasickness, but in a few seconds I was leaning over the rail. Then I staggered to my berth and flopped. For thirty hours, during the entire trip, I never moved. I didn't care how many submarines attacked us. The more the better. With two exceptions every one was ill. England ought to make money out of those trips. No one ate a mouthful.

Not until we were steaming into a Scottish harbor did I have strength to rise. Then I crawled on deck. It was nine in the evening and very dark. Only a few lights shone along the waterfront. But the smell of England came to my nostrils. The air was soft, the bleakness of Norway had vanished. The smoke from soft coal fires poured from the funnels. Something within me broke. The strain was over. I was safe at last. Here people spoke my language....

To reach France the channel had to be crossed. It was full moon, a bad time for crossing. A time when submarines reap their harvest. They see and cannot be seen. But the trip was short. I spent the night on deck, wrapped in a blanket. In the morning we were in Havre. Old men in blue blouses helped us disembark. The broad streets were lined with little sidewalk cafes. I was in the land of friendliness and charm. But the cafes and streets were deserted. Companies of soldiers marched past and little children and old men walked the streets. The train from Havre to Paris was packed with soldiers. I had suddenly been flung into the world's war. Until then I had seen little of war. In the countries through which I had traveled, except England, there had been but three topics of conversation, food, clothes and heat; how to live without freezing or starving. But here it was different. The battle field was a few miles away. Hospital trains moved back and forth. The newspapers had flaring headlines. Women in black filled the land. Yet curiously enough in this land of conflict the civil population throve....

CONCLUSION
A Dream

I sailed for home in a French boat. It left from the South of France. There was a thin, drizzly rain. The sea looked gray and desolate. We paused at the outer harbor for gun practice. For a day we attacked imaginary submarines. The long wait was varied by a life-saving drill. We strapped on life preservers and hurried to our respective life boats. Cabin passengers and steerage mingled indiscriminately. War travel removes social barriers. Our boat was a second-class steamer, but today one takes any boat gratefully. The cabin passengers consisted of the Countess De Breyas and her sister, 500 Spanish day laborers, some French and Italian officers and a dozen American Y.M.C.A. men. Silk sweaters and ragged coats, white sport shoes and clumsy leather clogs walked side by side. As we looked into each other's eyes there was but one question in our thoughts. "Are you afraid of submarines?" "Are you a free man or a coward?" In my cabin I found for room-mate a fashionable French dressmaker, a gay little person without purpose or plan in life, an outrageous flirt: but she had charm and a bit of inner serenity that shone out under the stress of danger.

I lay in bed in the morning and watched her dress. It was as good as a play. The art with which she powdered her nose, the gay little song when she jumped out of bed, her saucy words. Submarines lost their terror. I picked up her tiny, high-heeled boot, and placed it beside my heelless rubber-soled boy's shoe. "Look," I said. She caught my meaning and laughed gayly. When she left the cabin I lay thinking. How different we were! How much we needed each other! I needed her charm, she my seriousness. And suddenly we symbolized the whole world, the difference between individuals, between groups of individuals and between nations. The need of each for each and the fundamental goodness hidden beneath every exterior. My trip around the world spread before me like a book.

I saw Japan, socially in the 16th century, struggling against autocratic power, and Russia fled into the 21st fighting the bloody fight of Revolution. I saw in each nation those who believed in democracy contending with those who believed in autocracy. I saw in each individual the fight of the spirit with the forces of greed. I remembered the words of an Englishman, a member of the British official staff, who journeyed out of Russia with me who had said: "The thing for England to do is to *combine with Germany and police Russia*," and I shuddered. And I thought of the words of a group of wealthy French people traveling in a first-class carriage who had said: "It's all very well this talk about democracy but America is going too far. The Czar was the best person in Russia and we might better have peace with the Kaiser than with the German people," and again I shuddered. But then I smiled, for a picture of an American boy, laying down the law to a British soldier, flashed before me. The boy had said: "I've come over to fight for democracy, and your king has got to go. Say, what's his last name anyway?" And I turned the pages of my imaginary book to the meeting of the English women in St. Martin-in-the-Fields the day they dedicated their hard-won suffrage to the service of the truth.

And beneath all the struggle and the differences, the good and the ill, I saw the spirit slowly emerging triumphant. And my own spirit arose, steadied and grew calm. When I went on deck we made preparation to put out to sea. A friendly gray cruiser dashed up beside us. Then it hurried on beckoning and challenging us to follow. All day we sped over the gray sea, the steamers so close to each other one could call from deck to deck. Then night came. Every port hole was darkened; not a glimmer of light showed on deck. To walk about was impossible. One bumped into chairs or felt the mysterious touch of another human wanderer. For long I leaned over the rail watching the cruiser, dimly outlined, as she rode by our side. She too was dark and mysterious. At last I gathered up my blankets and wrapping them about me stretched out in my steamer chair. By my side lay my life preserver. But fear had gone out of my heart and wonder entered in. Wonder at this great onrushing world with its incessant upward striving. All night I lay there and sometimes I slept and when I slept I dreamed.

In a far distant country I saw a group of women gathered about a council table. And the women came from all lands, and they were of all ages and nationalities. But in the eyes of each was understanding, tenderness, and inner vision. And their talk was of children, of the children of their day and of the race to come. And no woman spoke of my children but only of our children. From their talk it grew plain that strife was still upon the earth. Kings had vanished, internationalism had come but class fought against class. From time to time, a man would burst into their council chamber and waving his arms shout, "Come, comrades, you must not sit here. We too have your ideals but this is a time for action, not ideals. Come, fight with us the bloody fight of revolution. Draw your sword and slay the monster greed." And from their midst some woman would rise and answer: "This man is right, class must fight against class. Those who have not must slay those who have. There is no other way to rid the earth of lust and greed." But wiser women shook their heads. They wept as the man and his sister went forth. They knew the high idealism in the heart of each but they knew the sword in their hands would in time breed again the greed and cruelty they sought to slay.

And one woman far down the council table rose and began to speak. Her body was frail, great circles lay beneath her eyes, but her spirit shone out in every gesture, so attuned was the inner and outer being that she seemed hardly more than a shining light. "We have come," she said, "to the final struggle. Up through the ages man has

CONCLUSION

toiled. Sometimes he made excursions into the material world, sometimes into the realms of the spirit. Each generation records his achievements. But in his onward march he used any means to gain his ends; he divorced body from spirit. He kept love in bondage. But we know that this is not the way, that ugly methods will turn and rend fine ends. The world for which we strive is one of love and it can be built only through love, through union of body and spirit, union of man with woman, of men with men and women with women and race with race. To women this is clear. Through us all new life passes. The tiny creature at our breast is more than a baby form. It is a bit of God, the temple of the spirit. This we must teach men; that life is sacred; that he may give life but must not take; that the body must be the instrument of the spirit; our physical acts the expression of the soul. Our revolutions and reforms must be based on fine deeds. When we are persecuted body as well as spirit must go dancing to jail. For only through the complete identification of the outer and inner world do we achieve mastery of earth, and then indeed may we seek new kingdoms."

And then I awoke, and I saw the stars had come out and the cruiser was plainly visible. And we sped on through the quiet night. The white foam dashed about us and the steamer rose and fell, and the ship's bells rang out, and I closed my eyes and slept again. And this time I dreamed I was in a land of sunshine. The sky was bluer than I had ever seen it. And about a pool danced some naked children. And drops of water stood on their firm and supple little bodies, and laughter shone in their eyes, and they tossed their golden curls and stretched their tiny hands to the sun, and tried to capture the sunbeams. And they were like the flowers, straight and beautiful, and they looked at each other with joy and wonder, and they knew no evil for body and spirit were one. And under a great tree where the sunlight filtered through the leaves sat a young man and a young woman. And their arms were about each other and they did not hide their love. They touched each other with reverence, for they were as gods to one another. The look in their eyes, the words of their mouth, the touch of their hands was sheer music; the singing music of the spirit, which pours itself out through the finger tips onto the keys of a piano. And I walked further on and I saw an older man and woman working together over an airship, and the light that came from them was blinding. For in this land with age, people grow ever more resplendent; for graven on the human form is the spiritual growth of the years. And I asked them what they were doing. And they said they were building an airship in which to sail to the stars. "You see," they said, "we have learned the secret of love, the union of all things, and now we know we no longer need to die. Already death has lost its sting. There is no tearing of the soul from the body; matter expresses only spirit and now we hope to sail away and not come back to earth again. Even as the worm bursts its chrysalis, and emerges a shining butterfly, so we, having made earth heaven, hope to spread our wings and fly into another world." Then I woke, and daylight had come. And the sunlight made a pathway on the waters, and the cruiser had turned back and was steaming toward France. We were far out at sea and each moment the danger from submarines grew less. And I looked at my fellow passengers with new interest. And in some I saw that the body had conquered the spirit, that their faces held coarse and sensual lines and blankness was in their eyes. But in others in the gesture of a hand, in the flash of an eye, in the laughter of a baby, I caught the body expressing the spirit. And the world became a new wonder, and I knew that the dream I had dreamed was a great truth.

INDEX

A-Club, xiii, xv
All Russian Congress of Soviets, 19, 35, 42n2, 46, 57n6, 58
All Russian League of Women's Enfranchisement, 70
All Russian Peasants Congress, 43
All Russian Soviet. *See* All Russian Congress of Soviets
Allies, xxi, 46n7, 59, 60
    aggressive designs of, 66
    Bolshevism will spread to lands of, 62
    don't join in Russian-German negotiations, 65
    don't support Bolsheviks, xxviii
    Germans drive wedge between Russians and, xxix
All-Russian Committee for the Salvation of the Motherland and the Revolution, 42n3
All-Russian League for Women's Equality, 71n4
America. *See* United States
American Union Against Militarism, xx, xxiii
anarchists, xi, 17n1, 41
Andreyevna, Maria Fyodorovna, xiv, xv, 27, 27n5, xvn27, 37, 38
aristocracy, xviii, 18, 28, 37, 51
    disguised in Red Cross uniform, xxvii, 26, 35
    estates taken from, 29, 45n5, 53
    Gorky takes pity on, 27n6
    school for, 19, 41
    titles abolished, xxvi, 21
Ashley, Jessie, xii
autocracy, xxviii, 35, 43
    of Germany, xxii, xxix
    of Japan, xxxiv, xxxv, 81
    of Soviet government, 38

Baldwin, Roger, xi, xviii, xxii, xxiii, xviiin40, xxiiin54

Beatty, Bessie, x, xxvi, xxvii, xxx
    on Bolshevik Revolution, xxiv
    courier for Bolsheviks, xxvn57
    on feminist movement in Russia, xxxi
    interviews Bolshevik women, xxxii
    member of Heterodoxy, xvi, xxv
    on Russian women's military service, xxxiv
    on Russia's allies, xxviii, xxix
    in Winter Palace, 25–26n3
Behind the Battle Line, ix, xxii, xxiv, xxv, xxxiv–xxxvii
    in Doty's autobiography, vii, x
    and Doty's independence, 18n2
    and Emmeline Pethick-Lawrence, xxxvi
    on Russian Revolution, vii, xxxv
    on Russian women, xxxiv
    on Russian working class, xxvii, 24n11
Beijing, China. *See* Peking, China
Berkman, Alexander, 17n1
Bochkareva, Maria, xxxiv
Bolshevik coup, vii, viii, xxv, xxxiv, viin2, 10n6, 48n9
    conditions in Russia during and after, 20n4
    Kamenev resigns after, 57n6
    Kerensky in no position to oppose, 13n9
    Women's Battalion members arrested after, 19n3
Bolshevik Revolution, viii, x, xxiv, 40n1, 42n3, 45, 48n9. *See also* Bolsheviks; Russian Revolution
    Beatty's and Bryant's accounts of, xxiv
    Doty in the midst of, xxii, xxxvii, viin2, 25
    Doty's accounts of, viii, viiin4
    former supporters condemn, 17n1
    peasant women support, 71, 75
    Reed's account of, 21n5
    Spiridonova's support of, 43n4
    YMCA representatives arrive at outset of, 10n6
Bolshevik Soviet, 42

Bolsheviks, xxxvi, 20, 25, 27, xxvn57, 78
  angry with aristocracy, 35
  arrest members of Women's Battalion, 19n3
  associated with immorality, 21n6
  attitudes about sex, xviii
  become dictators, xxvii, 19, 23, 33, 52, 72
  capture the government, 69
  Chernov and Zeretelli, 46
  Chinese support, 9n4
  composed of peasants, 52
  control central government, 41
  decrees of, xxvi, 21, 42n2
  delay Constituent Assembly meeting, 45n6
  distrust Minister of Finance, 32
  Don Cossacks rally against, 46n7
  don't hold to their ideal, 68
  don't need capitalistic luxury, 77
  Doty serves as courier for, xxvn57, 76
  Doty's feelings about, xxvii, xxviii, 22n7, 79
  elected to Duma, 49
  extreme left of Socialists, 17
  Gorky's relationship to, 27n6, 37
  government of, 61, 63, 66, 70, 74, 75
  grow in power, 22
  interventions on behalf of women, xxxiii
  Kaiser meets with, 55, 56
  Kamenev prominent leader of, 57n6
  keep execution secret, 25n1, 29n8
  Kollontai controversial among, 72n5
  Konavello denounces, 38
  Kronstadt sailors rebel against, 17n1
  Kühlmann aids, 65n16
  launch coup, vii, xxxiv, viin2, 10n6, 13n9
  Lenin and Trotsky leaders of, 48n9
  majority of population is, 44
  make peace with Germany, 55n3
  mobs, 30
  The Nation (London) spreads terror of, 22n9
  Novaya Zhizn publishes views of, 37n7
  officials of, 62
  Panina caught in machine of, 73
  in peace negotiations with Germany, 59n9
  peace parade of, 64
  at Peasants' Congress, 51
  as People's Commissars, 42
  period of control, 27n7
  politics of, x
  power of, xxv, 14, 43
  program of, xxxii
  promise to unite Assembly, 48
  propaganda of, 20n4
  Reed and Bryant support, 22n10
  sign peace treaty, xxix, 67
  in Smolny Institute, 18, 40, 40n1
  in Social Democratic Workers' Party, 33n3
  as Social Democrats, xv, viiin3
  Socialist Revolutionaries contend for power with, xiii, 43–44n4, 50n10
  take banks, 26
  take over Winter Palace, 42n2
  take Petrograd, 19
  in throes of their struggle, 24
  Ukrainian allegiances shift to, 66n18
  unfriendly to Constituent Assembly, 45
  violent tendencies of, xxiv, 72
  working women side with, 71
Bolshevism, 46n7, 62
bourgeoisie, 18, 45, 50, 61
  Americans in Russia seen as, 14
  are on underside of Russian society, 19
  are unrepresented in Soviets, 44
  Doty's view of, xxvi, xxvii, 51
  half of US is, 31
  imprisoned, 67
  march in parade, 47
  overthrown, 59
  proletariat victorious over, 49
  sided with Kerensky, 71
Bramson, L. M., 34, 34n4
Breshkovskaya, Catherine, xiii, xiv, xxxii, 71
Brest-Litovsk, Treaty of, xxix, 56, 60, 63, 65, 66
  Bolsheviks and Socialist Revolutionaries disagree over, 50n10
  Hoffman a negotiator of, 59n8
  and Kamenev, 57, 57n6
  Mirbach-Harff participates in, 63n15
  reasons Russians agree to, 55
  terms of, 55n4
Bryant, Louise, xxvi, 21n5, 25n3, xxvn57, 73n7
  account of Russian Revolution, x, xxiv
  describes Russian children, xxxiii
  discusses Russian women more than Doty, xxx
  discusses Women's Battalion of Death, xxxiv

in Heterodoxy, xvi
interviews leading Bolshevik women, xxxii
pro-Bolshevik, xxv, 22n10
recounts travels to and from Russia, xxxvn93

capitalists, 31, 53, 60, 77
  Americans in Russia seen as, 14
  arrested, 67
  Doty not, 20
  go regularly to bed, 26
  hatch plots for counter-revolution, 46
  judged in court, 30n1
  land taken from, 52
  march in parade, 47
  must be beheaded, 32, 36
  Petrograd hotels are, 18
  put hope in Constituent Assembly, 45
  on underside of Russian society, 19
  unrepresented in Soviets, 44
Central Powers, 42, 44, 54n1, 55n3, 56, 59
Chernov, Victor, 44, 46, 48, 51, 52
  arrest of, 43n4, 67
  elected president of All Russian Peasants Congress, 43
  elected president of Constituent Assembly, 47
China and Chinese, 5, 6, 8, 8n1, 25, 27
  democratic spirit of, 9n5
  discussed in *Behind the Battle Line*, ix, xxxiv
  Doty in, 7
  Doty trusts, 9
  fear Europeans, 7
  role in February Revolution, 9n4
civil war, Russian, 10n6, 17n1, 27n6, 46n7, 49
conservatives, xxxv, 3–4, 45, 46, 72, 72n6
Constituent Assembly, 34, 47, 48, 49, 72, 74n8, 75
  battle over, 45n6
  Bramson a delegate to, 34n4
  Chernov and Zeretelli talk at, 46
  doesn't reflect opinion of the masses, 52
  elected based on universal suffrage, 70, 71
  must recognize Soviet power, 64
  represents all classes, 45
  Schreider's speech about, 42, 43
Corea. *See* Korea
correspondents. *See* journalists
Cossacks, 9, 12n7, 42n3, 46, 46n7, 64

Doty shares train compartment with, xxv, 10
Council of Workingmen and Soldiers, 35, 70, 71
counter-revolution, 19, 20, 43, 48, 50, 53
  Kadets want, 49
  monarchists and capitalists want, 22n9, 46
  Panina not part of, 74
  Purishkevich arrested for participating in, 35n5
coup. *See* Bolshevik coup
czar. *See* tsars
czarinas. *See* tsarinas

Denikin, Anton, 46n7
District Soviets, 44. *See also* Soviets
Dorr, Rheta Childe, xvi, xxiv
Doty, Madeleine Z., ix, 6f, 11f, 12n7
  accounts of Bolshevik Revolution, viiin4
  on Andreyeva, xxx, 27n5
  anti-Semitism of, 15n11
  arrives in Petrograd, viin2, ixn7
  on Bolshevik-Germany treaty, 55n3, 55n4
  commitment to peace, xviii, xxxvii
  contact with YMCA, 10n6
  contempt for monarchists and liberals, 22n7
  courier for Bolsheviks, xxvn57, 76
  critical of Bolshevik methods, xxviii, xxix, xxxvi
  feelings about Bolsheviks, xviii
  feelings about bourgeoisie and nobility, xxvii, 26
  feelings about German militarism, xviii
  feels like Alice in Wonderland in Russia, viii, x, viiin4, 22, 36
  feminist activism of, xvii, xxii, xxxvii, 69n1
  friendship with Emmeline Pethick-Lawrence, xxxvi
  gives birth outside marriage, xviiin18, xviiin37
  on Gorky, 27n6
  in Heterodoxy, xviin34
  history of, x–xiv
  on imperial family, 29n8
  impression of Lenin, xxvi
  involvement with Phillips, xvii–xviii
  justice activism of, xi, xviii, xix
  on Kaiserling, 62n14
  on Kollontai, 72n1

launches journalism career, xv
in midst of Bolshevik Revolution, xxxvii
more comfortable in China than Japan, 9n5
peace activism of, xx, xxi, xxii, xxiii, xxxvi
on Peasant Assembly, 43n4
permit to enter Smolny Institute, 40f
as progressive maternalist, xviiin39
with Reed, 21n5
relationship with Baldwin, xxii–xxiii
relationship with Bryant, 22n10
relies on men's help in Russia, xxv
on Russian divorce, 21n6
on Russian Revolution, viii, xxiv, xxvi, xn15, 24n11
on Russian women, xxxi, xxxii, xxxiii, xxxiv, 14n10, 69n1, 70n2
in Smolny Institute, 40n1
social activism of, xi, xvi, xviii, xix
on suffrage, 38n8
in suffrage parade, xxif
tones down discussion of violence, 17–18n2, 22n8
travel to and from Russia, xxxv
travels in Europe, 3n1
use of term "Social Democrat," 33n3
views of Woodrow Wilson, 32n2
on Women's Battalion of Death, 19n3
world travel of, 76n1
writes *Behind the Battle Line*, vii
Dumas, 34, 44, 48, 49, 52, 59n9
dissolved, 43, 46n8, 47
Doty at, 51
of Petrograd, 42, 42n3

Eastman, Crystal, xii, xvi, xx, xxiii
East/West differences, 8, 8n2, 68
customs, 6
religion, 10n6
women, xxxi, 71
England and the English, 7, 62, 66, 76, 81
challenges Germany, 61
Doty's travels in, 3n1, 80
Doty's writings on, ix, xxii, xxxiv, xxxvi, xxxvii
feminists in, xvi, xxx, 38n8
London, ix, xxxvi
in Petrograd, 63
women of, viii

Equality League of Self-Supporting Women, xvi
Executive Committee of the Petrograd Soviet, 13n9

February Revolution, xxiv, 9n4, 10n6, 17, 43n4, 46nn7–8, 69n1
feminism and feminists, xii, xxiii, xxv
Alexandra Kollontai, 72n5
and anti-Semitism, xxx
of Doty, ix–x, xi, xvi, xvii
Doty's view of Russians, xxxvii, 69n1
movements in Russia, 70, 70n2
during Russian Revolution, xxxi, xxxii, 69
throughout world, xxxv
Figner, Vera, 70, 70n3, 71
Fortress of Peter and Paul, 27, 33, 34, 38, 49, 75
dire deeds occur in, 30
Doty visits, 31, 32
emotional atmosphere of, 37
jailers of, 36
ministers imprisoned in, 19, 37
Spiridonova imprisoned in, 74
use of, 27n7
France and the French, viii, xxii, 3n1, 62, 66
Doty's travels in, 80, 81, 83
Doty's writings on, ix, xxxiv
in Petrograd, 63
Ukraine accepts money from, 66

Germany and Germans, xxii, 38, 81, 82
advance into Belgium, 60n10
Alfred Peter Friedrich von Tirpitz, 61n13
armies in Russia, 8n3
autocracy of, xxii, xxix
Baron Kaiserling, 60n12
compared to Sweden, 78
conditions in worsen, 56
Count Georg von Hertling, 58n7
delegation in Petrograd, 60, 61, 62, 63, 64
Doty's travels in, xviii, 3n1, 33n3
Doty's views of, xviii
Doty's writings on, ix, xviii
invades Europe, 80
invades Russia, 51, 54
involvement in World War I, 56n5
Lenin accepts terms of, 67n19
militarism of, xxvi, 17, 24

occupies Ukraine, 66n18
prejudices of, xxx
propaganda of, 31
refugees from in Stockholm, 79
relations with Russia, xxix, 35, 59nn8–9, 67, 68
Richard von Kühlmann, 65n16
Russia wants revolution in, xxix, 55, 61, 66, 68
Russian Soviet appeals to people of, 65
spies in Smolny Institute, 41
take Russian prisoners, 13
Treaty of Brest-Litovsk, 55nn3–4, 57
view of Russia, 58, 59
Wilhelm Graf von Mirbach-Harff, 63n15
Goldman, Emma, xvi, 17n1
Good Housekeeping, viii, ix, xxii, xxiii, xxxv
Gorky, Maxim, xivf, xix, 39, 73
  American support of, xiii
  in danger of imprisonment, xxxv, 3, 26–27
  Doty visits, 37, 38
  Doty's writings on, xiv
  establishes *Novaya Zhizn*, 37n7
  relationship to Bolsheviks, 27nn6
  relationship with Andreyevna, 27nn5, xvn27
  visits US, xv
Great Britain. *See* England and the English

Harbin/Shenyang, China, xxv, 8, 8n1, 9, 9n4
Harding, Florence, xxxv, 6f
Heterodoxy (club), xvi–xvii, xxv, xvin33, xviin34
Hoffman, Max, 56, 59, 59n8

intellectuals, 13n9, 27n6, 37, 46, 47, 73
  side with Kerensky, 71
  on underside of Russian society, 19
  unrepresented in Soviets, 44
Intercollegiate Socialist Society, xvi
International Women's Day, 69n1

Japan, ix, xxxiv, 6f, 9, 9n5, 13
  Doty's travels in, 5–6, 8, 25
  Doty's writings on, xxxv
  relations with China and Russia, 8n1
  struggles against autocratic power, 81
  women of, 3
Jews, xii, xiii, xxii, xxiii, 15, 48n9

anti-Semitism, 15n11, 35n5
Kishinev Massacre, xxx
journalists, xxiv, xn15, 47, 58
  American, 10, 12, 22, 22n10, 25, xvn27
  American women in Russia, xxxiii
  Bessie Beatty, xvi
  David Graham Phillips, xvii
  Jessie Lloyd O'Connor, 45n5
  John Reed, 21
  life of, 76
  Louise Bryant, xvi, 21n5
  Madeleine Z. Doty, xi, xviii, xx, xviin34, 41
  Western women, viii, x, xiii, xxiv, xxv
July Days, 10n6, 13n9

Kadets, 22, 22n7, 31, 32n2, 46n8, 51, 52
  arrests of, 47
  Countess Panina, xxxii
  declared enemies of the people, 43n4, 45, 48, 49, 50, 64
  fragile coalition of liberals, viii
  Kadet Corps, 19
  Kerensky liaison between socialist intellectuals and, 13n9
  members of Petrograd Municipal Duma, 42
  as officials, 43
Kaiser, 41, 58, 59, 61, 82
  and Brest-Litovsk, treaty, xxix, 55, 56
Kaiserling, Count Baron, 60, 60n12, 61, 62, 62n14
Kaledin, Aleksei M., 46, 46n7. *See also* Kaledinists
Kaledinists, 50
Kamenev, Lev. B., 57, 57n6, 58, 65, 66
Kerensky, Alexander, 25n1, 42, 42n3, 44, 50, 71
  attempts to quell uprising, viii, viin2
  forced into exile, viiin2
  moderates support, xxvii
  in power, 70, 73
  Provisional Government under, 18
  role in Russian Revolution, 13n9
  rumors about, 12, 14
Kollontai, Alexandra, xviii, 58, 72nn5–6, 73
  articulates comradely love, xxii
  Bolshevik leader, xxviii
  Doty interviews, xxxii
  given government position, 72

Konovalov, Alexander I., 37, 37n6, 38
Korea, 6, 9n5, 25
Kornilov, Lavr, 13n9, 46n7
Kremlin, 26, 27, 28
Kronstadt, Russia, 17, 17n1, 23, 27n6, 38

law, xiii, xxii, xxvi, 21, 34, 42, 52
laws, xxxiii, 24n11, 78
Left SRs, 43–44n4, 63n15
Lenin, Vladimir, 42n2, 50, 63
   accepts German terms, 67n19
   Bolshevik leader, 48n9
   Chernov calls for ejection of, 51
   decides to execute Romanovs, 25n1
   Doty swept up by presence of, xxvi
   expects German revolution, xxix
   Kamenev disagrees with, 57n6, 59n9
   launches coup against Provisional Government, vii, 13n9
   sends manifesto to German trenches, 57
   speeches of, 48, 49, 52
   Treaty of Brest-Litovsk, 55n4
   views published in *Novaya Zhizn*, 37n7
Leopold, Prince of Bavaria, 56, 65
Liberal Club, xvi
liberals. *See* Kadets
Liebknecht, Karl, xxviii, 56, 56n5, 57, 59, 67
Luxemburg, Rosa, 56n5, 59

Marxism, xiii, 13n9, 48n9, 55, 56n5
Mensheviks, viiin3, 13, 33n3, 37n7, 43, 48n9
mobs, 30, 64
monarchists, 19, 25n1, 44
   Doty's contempt for, 22n7
   hatch plots for counter-revolution, 46
   indicted, 37
   resistance of, 22
   spread terror of Bolsheviks, 22n9
   Vladimir M. Purishkevich, xxvii, 35
Moscow, Russia, ix, xxvii, 14, 26, 27, 45n5, 63n15
Mukden, China, 7, 8, 8n1

Nation, The (London), xxvii, xxxi, xxxv, 17–18n2, 21n5, 22n10, 24n11
National Woman's Party, xxiv, 38n8
Nicholas II, 25n1, 29, 59n9, 61. *See also* tsars
nobility, xxvii, 26, 28, 29, 40n1, 70n3. *See also* aristocracy

Noradnyi Dom, xxxii, 73, 74
Novaya Zhizn, 37, 37n7, 39

O'Connor, Jessie Lloyd, 45n5
October Revolution. *See* Bolshevik Revolution

Panin, Countess. *See* Panina, Countess
Panina, Countess, xxxii, 72n5, 73, 74, 74n8, 75
Pankhurst, Christabel, xx
peace, xxxvi, 57, 59, 60, 61, 63, 65, 82
   activism, xx–xxii, xxiii, xxxvi
   Bolshevik peace parade, 64
   Central Powers want, 56
   and Constituent Assembly, 47
   Doty on, xxviii
   Doty's commitment to, xi, xviii, xxxvii
   German proposals for, 66
   international women's peace gathering, 3n1
   Kaiser's, xxix
   Russian people want, 18
   between Russians and Bolsheviks, 55n3
   between Russians and Germans, 55, 55n3, 58, 59n9, 67
   undemocratic terms of, 68, 75
peace negotiations, xxviii, 54n1, 58, 59, 59n9, 65, 65n16. *See also* Brest-Litovsk, Treaty of
Peasants Congress, 43, 44, 50, 51, 58
Peking, China, 5, 7, 8, 27
People's Commissars, 42, 48, 48n9, 49, 64
Pethick-Lawrence, Emmeline, xxxvi
Petrograd. *See* St. Petersburg, Russia
Phelps, J. G., xiii
Phillips, David Graham, xvii, xviii, xix
plebeians, 25, 62
populists, viiin3, 48n9, 50n10
Pouriskevitch. *See* Purishkevich, Vladimir M.
prisoners, 13, 33, 38, 60
   Countess Panina, 75
   Doty interviews, 32
   Germans take, 13
   Irakli Zeretelli, 46
   Lev. B. Kamenev, 57n6
   Maria Spiridonova, 43n4
   ministers as, 19, 32, 37
   political, xii, 27n7
   released, 30
   royal, 56
   Social Democrats as, 33

treatment of, 34, 39
trials of, 35, 36, 37
prisons, xii, 27, 67, 71. *See also* Fortress of Peter and Paul
   in Germany, 54
   reform of, xix
   reform of in US, xi
   in Siberia, 43n4, 46n8
proletariat, xxvi, 19, 47, 48, 49, 51, 57
Provisional Government, 35n5, 37n6, 42, 71
   American support of, 10n6
   coup against, vii
   under Kerensky, 18
   in power, 13n9, 70, 73
   socialistic values of, xxiv
   struggles to maintain control, viii
   use of Fortress of Peter and Paul under, 27n7
   Winter Palace is seat of, 25n3
   Women's Battalion of Death defends, xxxiv
Purishkevich, Vladimir M., xxvii, 35, 35n5, 36, 37

Rasputin, 35, 35n5
Rauh, Ida, xii, xiii
Red Army, 25n3, 48n9
Red Guard, 23, 35n5, 58, 59
Red Terror, 27n6
Reed, John, xxv, 21, 21n5, 22n10
reporters. *See* journalists
Revolution of 1905, xiii, 35n5, 42n2, 48n9
Revolution of 1917, vii, xiii, viin2, 48n9, 57n6, 69
Revolutionary Tribunal, 30, 34, 35n5, 49, 74
revolutionists and revolutionaries, 30, 50, 55, 63
   Alexandra Kollontai, 72
   Angelica Balabanov, 73n7
   Germans as, 54
   in Japan, xxxv, 3
   Lev. B. Kamenev, 57n6
   Maria Spiridonova, 73
   Maxim Gorky, xiv
   Russian women as, xxxii
   Vera Figner, 70n3
Right SRs, 43n4. *See also* Socialist Revolutionaries
Romanovs, 25n1, 54. *See also* tsars

Russian Revolution, 17n1, 50, 67. *See also* Bolshevik Revolution
   brought legal changes for women, 14n10
   causes of, 59
   defining moment in, 25n3
   Doty downplays violence of, 22n8
   Doty's accounts of, vii, ix, x, xxv, xxvii, 22n10
   Doty's experience of, xxxvii, 9, ixn15, 23
   Doty's interest in, xi
   Doty's support for, 24n11
   Doty's travels to and from, xxii
   Doty's views of, xxvi
   early days of, 30
   evidence of in St. Petersburg, 15, 17
   Gorky icon of, 27n6
   popular conceptions of, xiv
   Revolutionary News Bureau reports on, xiii
   Russian women in, 69, 69n1, 75
   spiritual regeneration from, 39
   Western women journalists covering, viii, xxiv
   "Women in the Revolution" (Beatty), xxxi
   women's suffrage coincides with, 38n8, 70
   and WWI, xxxv
   YMCA's influence in Russia during, 10n6
Russians, xxiii, 12, 27n6
   antagonistic against German government, 55
   attitudes about sex, 12n8
   can think and talk, 32, 54, 79
   characteristics of, 17, 20, 23, 24, 54, 56, 64
   German delegation unlike, 54
   Lenin claims Constituent Assembly doesn't reflect opinion of, 52
   pent up anger of, 22n8
   refugees from in Stockholm, 79
   revengeful force of, 38
   used to eccentricities and informalities, 58
   views of US, 31
   WWI made into refugees, 8n2
Russo-Japanese War, 8n1

sex and romantic relationships, xi, xii, 12n8
   Bolshevik attitudes about, xviii, 72n5
   Doty's attitudes about, xii, xiv, xvii, xviii
Shenyang/Harbin, China, xxv, 8, 8n1, 9, 9n4
Shishkina-Yavein, Poliksena, 71, 71n4

Short Rations, ix, xxii, xxv, 3n1
Siberia, 8n1, 43n4, 68, 70, 73
   Doty's travels in, 8, 18, 25
   peasants exiled to, xiv
   Romanovs sent to, 25n1
   Russian women exiled to, xxxii, 69
   women of, xxxiii, 13, 14
Smith College, xi, xii, xv, xxiii, xn15, 45n5
Smolny Institute, 18, 19, 40, 40f, 73
   German spies could enter, 41
   indignation meeting held at, 65, 66
   origins of, 40n1
   Trotsky and Lenin speak at, 49
Social Democratic Workers' Party, 33n3
Social Democrats, 14, 33, 37n7, 48n9
   Bolshevik faction of, xv
   Chernov, 43
   German, xxviii, 33n3, 55, 56n5, 59, 65, 67
   Liebknecht, 56n5, 59
   Luxemberg, 59
   Mensheviks moderate wing of, 13n9
   predecessors to Bolsheviks, 27n6
   Socialist Revolutionaries more moderate than, viii
   Zetkin, 59
social welfare, xxxi, 3n3, 23, 69
   for children, xviii, xxi
   minister of, xxxii, 72, 72n5
socialism and socialists, xiii, 21, 37, 41, 42, 42n3, 57–58
   Alexander Kerensky, viii, 13n9
   are arrested, 52
   Bolshevik are extreme left of, 17
   Bolsheviks arrest, xxix, 33
   in Constituent Assembly, 46, 50
   Crystal Eastman, xii
   Doty described as, xxiii
   Doty's involvement with, xi, xvi
   gather in Smolny Institute, 41
   German, 55, 56, 59, 63, 67
   Irakli Zeretelli, 46n8
   Jessie Lloyd O'Connor, 45n5
   John Martin, xv
   join in resistance to Bolshevik operations, 42n2
   Karl Liebknecht, 56n5
   oppose German militarism, 33n3
   refuse to recognize new government, 43
   University Settlement is haven for, xiii

Socialist Revolutionaries, viii, xiii, viiin3, 13n9, 41, 43n4, 50n10. *See also* Left SRs
Society's Misfits, xix
Soviet Union, x, xxxii, 27n6
Soviets, 46, 53, 62, 64, 65, 66, 67
   agent of, 48n9
   debates in, 49
   Democratic peace proposals of, 55
   Germany recognizes, 68
   government of, 38
   Kadets didn't join, 43
   marriage laws of, xxxiii
   Municipal Duma refuses to recognize, 42
   of Petrograd, 13n9
   power of, 52
   practices of, xxii–xxiii
   Russian Congress, 41
   take place of Dumas and Zemstvos, 44
Spiridonova, Maria, xxviii, 43, 51, 58, 72, 73n7
   Doty interviews, xxxii
   legendary among peasants, 43n4
   on women, 73
SRs, 13n9, 50n10. *See also* Left SRs; Socialist Revolutionaries
St. Petersburg, Russia, 25n1, 26, 58, 67
   All Russian Peasants Congress in, 43
   American Military Control in, 30
   Bolsheviks take, 19
   campfires burning in, 31
   a city of working people, 22, 70, 71
   Constituent Assembly in, 47, 48
   Cossacks were to march on, 46
   Doty is ill in, xxv
   Doty leaves, 76
   Doty travels to, vii, ix, xxiv, xxx, xxxiii, ixn7, 18n2
   Doty's arrival to, xxvi, viin2, ixn7, 8, 9, 12, 16
   foreigners experienced hardship in, 20
   German delegation in, xxviii, 60, 63
   Germans march on, xxix, 54
   "How I Came to Petrograd" (Doty), 11f
   Kaiserling in, 61
   Kerensky flees, viiin2
   Lenin and Trotsky in, 57
   life in difficult for a stranger, 18
   Mayak opens in, 10n6
   Noradny Dome, xxxi, xxxii

INDEX

not peaceful, 21
Panina tried in, 74, 75
Petrograd City Duma, 42, 42n3
revolution in, 15, 17
Revolutionary News Bureau begun in, xiii
rioting and bloodshed in, 14
riots of the February Revolution in, 17n1
rumors about, 13
Smolny Institute, 40, 40n1
Stalin, Joseph, 44n4, 48n9, 57n6
Stokes, Rose Pastor, xvii
Stolypin, Pyotr, 46n8
Strunsky Walling, Anna, xiii
suffragists and suffragettes, xii, xvi, xx, xxif, xxxvi, 38, 38n8. *See also* women's suffrage

Tereshchenko, Mikhail I., 37, 37n6
terrorists, xxxii, viiin3, 70n3
Treaty of Brest-Litovsk. *See* Brest-Litovsk, Treaty of
Trotsky, Leon, xxviii, 41, 62
  causes reversion to authoritarianism, 42n2
  considered a man of affairs, 63
  defends decrees, 49
  involvement in Treaty of Brest-Litovsk, 55n4, 59n9
  Kamenev falls out of favor with, 57n6
  no war no peace strategy, xxix
  presiding over All Russian Soviet, 19
  second in command of Bolsheviks, 48n9
  speeches of, 48, 50, 58, 67
  taunted, 52
  writes manifesto for German soldiers, 57
tsarinas, 25, 26, 28, 29n8, 40n1. *See also* aristocracy
tsars, xxxv, 25, 53, 55, 61. *See also* aristocracy
  abdication of, vii
  abuses under, 30
  Alexander II, 70n3
  apartments of, 28
  army of, 35
  dictatorship of, xiv, 33, 72
  execution of family, 29n8
  fall of, xxxiii
  French view of, 82
  Jews restricted under, xxx
  looting former home of, 23
  Nicholas II, 13n9, 25n1, 25n3, 29
  overthrowing of, xxxvii, 59

  regimes of, viii, viiin3
  Romanovs, 54
  socialists under, 52
  Spiridonova's abuse under, 73

Ukraine, 55n4, 65, 66, 66n18
United States, 10n6, 20, 47, 58, 68
  American Embassy, 58, 76
  anti-Semitism expressed in, xxx
  Bolshevik propaganda in, 20n4
  Breshkovsky tours, xiii
  Bryant's readers in, 22n10
  "darkest Russia" popularly used in, 8n2
  Doty dies in, xxiii–xxiv
  Doty's journey from and back to, xxxv
  Doty's readers in, 21n6, 22n8
  Doty's travels in, xvii, xxxiv
  enters WWI, xxii
  Figner legendary in, 70, 70n3
  French view of, 82
  Germany doesn't fear, 61
  Gorky travels to, xiv, xivf, xv, 27n6
  Greenwich Village, xi
  journalists from, xxiv, 10, 12, xn15, 22, 22n10, 25
  news of Russian Revolution in, xviii
  Pankhurst travels to, xx–xxi
  Russian views of, 62
  Russian women legendary in, xxxii
  Russians deserve support of, xxvii, 24
  Russians' interest in, 31, 32, 33
  suffragists in, 38n8
  views of Russia, 8n2
  women of, x, xviii, xxxii, xxxiii, 38n8
  Young Women's Christian Association in, 3n3
US. *See* United States

von Czernin, Otto, 59, 59n8
von Hertling, Count George, 58, 58n7
von Kühlmann, Richard, 65, 65n16
von Mirbach-Harff, Wilhelm Graf, 63, 63n15, 67
von Tirpitz, Alfred Peter Friedrich, 61, 61n13
Vorse, Mary Heaton, xiii

Walling, William English, xiii
WILPF. *See* Women's International League for Peace and Freedom

Wilson, Woodrow, xxxvi, 10n6, 31, 32n2
Winter Palace, 23, 25, 26n3, 31, 50
   Bolshevik takeover of, 42n2
   falls, 13n9
   Provisional Government at, xxxiv, 18, 25n3
   storming of, xxv
   Women's Battalion of Death guards, 19, 19n3
Woman Suffrage League, 71
women, xiii, xvi, 21n5, 25, xviin34, 41, 45n5
   activism of, xxxvi
   African American, xvii
   American, x, xviii, xxxii, xxxiii, 38n8
   and romantic relationships, xi
   anti-Semitism of, xxx
   appeal of Russian Revolution to, vii
   as travelers during Russian war, 26
   attitudes toward Bolshevik Revolution, 71
   Bolshevik, xxxii, 72
   careers for, xi
   changes for due to the Revolution, 14n10
   considered more principled than men, 73n7
   Doty's view of, xxxv, xxxvii, 82–83
   English, xxxvi, 38n8, 72, 82
   equality with men, 14
   Essentialist ideas about, xx
   French, viii
   in government service, 72
   history of, xn15
   and institutionalized violence, xx
   involvement in Russian wars, xxxi, 69n1
   Japanese, xxxiv, 3
   journalists, viii, xv, xxiv, xxv, xxxiii, xn15
   members of Heterodoxy, xvi–xvii
   military service of, 19n3
   modern, vii, xi, xviii, xxxiii, 3, 3n2
   political discussions of, ix
   in Red Cross, xvii, 35, 73
   relationships with men, xvii, 69, 83
   revolutionize women's position in Russia, xxxii–xxxiii
   rights activism, xx
   rights of, xxxi, xxxii, xxxiii
   role in new order, 4
   role in Russian Revolution, 70, 72, 75
   Siberian, xxxiii, 70
   situation of during Russian war, xxx
   study history, x
   support allied war effort, xxi
   support of Bolsheviks, xxxiv
   view of world war, viii
   Western, viii, x, xxiv, xxxii
   women's movements, xxx
   write about Russian war, vii, xxiv, xxv
   writers, viii, xvii, xxiii
women, Russian, viii, xvii, xxx, xxxi, xxxii, xxxiv
   activism of, 69n1
   attitudes toward Bolshevik Revolution, 73, 82
   attributes of, 73
   considered conservative, 72n6
   Doty's study of, xxxi–xxxii, 24n11, 69
   equality with men, 14, 14n10
   idealism of, 73
   in military service, xxxiv
   position of, 69
   in Red Cross, 26
   role in Russia's future, 75
   in Russian Revolution, xxxi–xxxii
   suffrage of, xxxiii, 70, 71
Women's Battalion of Death, xxxiv, 19, 19n3
Women's International League for Peace and Freedom, xxi, xxii
Women's International Peace Convention, xxi
Women's Peace Party, xx, xxi, xxxvi, 22n10
Women's Social and Political Union, 38n8
women's suffrage, xi, xvi, xx, xxii, xxiv, xxxvi, 69
   Doty on, 38n8
   during Russian Revolution, 70
   suffrage parade, xxif
World War I, viii, xx, xxiv, xxxv, 55, 56n5, 59n8
   creates Russian refugees, 8n2
   Doty on, ix
   in France, 80
   Woodrow Wilson decides to enter, 10n6
WPP. *See* Women's Peace Party

YMCA, 10, 10n6, 12, 77, 78, 81
Yokohama, Japan, ix, 5
Young Women's Christian Association, xxxv, 3, 3n3

Zalkind, Ivan, 62
Zeretelli, Irakli, 46, 46n8
Zetkin, Clara, xxviii, 56n5, 59

www.ingramcontent.com/pod-product-compliance
Lightning Source LLC
Chambersburg PA
CBHW032028230426

43671CB00005B/243